The Values of American Teachers

How Teachers' Values Help Stabilize Unsteady Democracy

Robert Slater

ROWMAN & LITTLEFIELD EDUCATION

A division of
ROWMAN & LITTLEFIELD
Lanham • Boulder • New York • Toronto • Plymouth, UK

Published by Rowman & Littlefield Education
A division of Rowman & Littlefield
4501 Forbes Boulevard, Suite 200, Lanham, Maryland 20706
www.rowman.com

10 Thornbury Road, Plymouth PL6 7PP, United Kingdom

British Library Cataloguing in Publication Information Available

Library of Congress Cataloging-in-Publication Data

Slater, Robert (Robert O.)
  The values of American teachers : how teachers' values help stabilize unsteady democracy / Robert Slater.
     pages cm
  ISBN 978-1-4758-0006-7 (cloth : alk. paper) — ISBN 978-1-4758-0007-4 (pbk. : alk. paper) — ISBN 978-1-4758-0008-1 (electronic) 1. Teachers—United States—Conduct of life. 2. Teaching—Moral and ethical aspects—United States. 3. Moral education—United States. 4. Democracy and education—United States. I. Title.
  LB1775.2.S63 2014
  371.102—dc23   2013023337

Printed in the United States of America

To My Children

Sebastian, Alex, Thomas, and Dorothy

Contents

Preface

This book is about the values of elementary- and secondary-school teachers. Teachers have lately become ground zero for federally influenced and state-led school-reform efforts. But while they find themselves once again at the center of things, it is not their values that are of interest but rather the *value they add* to student performance on standardized tests. "Value-added" teacher assessment is sweeping across the United States now.

Value-added teacher assessment is an effort to measure teacher quality by linking it to improvement in students' test scores. The "good" teachers are those who add value by increasing their students' scores from one year to the next. The basic logic behind this value-added approach is that, all things being equal, the greater the gain or "growth" in student scores during a given period, the more effective or higher the quality of the teacher.

Now, teachers do add value when they enable students to increase their performance on standardized tests, but this is not the only and not even the most important value they add. A major point of this book—one that arises out of analysis of national data on America and Americans—is that an equally if not more important value added by teachers is the contribution they make to the stabilization of democracy. This is particularly the case for democracy in America but it probably holds for other democracies as well.

Teachers' values are especially important in our modern democracies, for democracy around the world appears to be increasingly unstable, as the sociologist Max Weber predicted it would be. These dynamic systems are inclined to go to self-destructive extremes as they rush headlong into the future. Teachers' values help to check this tendency and stabilize these imbalanced-prone societies, and this stabilizing effect is an important value they add to the society as a whole.

The stabilizing effect that the data suggest teachers have on democracy is, however, a value added that has gone largely unnoticed and for which teachers have not been given the credit they deserve. Most if not all of the attention these days is being paid to the direct effects they have on test scores in science, mathematics, reading, and social studies. But their indirect effects on the stability of democracy—some of which are discussed in detail here—are just as important, if not more so, than their effects on test scores. Indeed, without these indirect effects, all the academic gains may be for naught.

Now, how, in general, do teachers stabilize democracy? More will be said on this in due course but stated briefly they appear to do so by serving as values "regulators," strengthening some values while repressing others, encouraging the development of one while discouraging that of another.

Which particular values teachers advance and which they check probably depends on the kind of society in which they find themselves. For example, in the United States, an advanced capitalist democracy, teachers tend to limit freedom. Of course freedom is, along with equality, one of every democracy's central values but in the U.S. case, at least, individual freedom happens to be a value that has a strong tendency, perhaps mainly for historical reasons, to be carried to excess. If the Occupy Movement and the gun-control debate in America show us nothing else, they show us this.[1]

It should come as no surprise that, when it comes to freedom, American teachers tend to be conservative. America's children daily carry into their classrooms the effects of a culture to which they have been exposed through television, the Internet, and the entertainment industry, a culture which, in the name and interest of freedom, has relatively few constraints. Freedom, in fact, not only enables this culture but it is also one of its central messages. It is, however, a freedom largely conveyed and understood as being able do whatever one wants—often without regard to the consequences for others.

Faced with the task of having to maintain orderly classrooms in a culture that encourages children to test the boundaries of individual freedom, teachers have to temper the ideas and understanding of liberty that children carry with them to school. In being conservative when it comes to the value of freedom, therefore, American teachers help to keep U.S. society—through the effects they have on its children's understanding of freedom—from taking individual liberty to extremes and thereby exacerbating the imbalances already at work.

Given what appears to be a greater fragility of democratic systems around the world, it is important to identify any and all of their sources of stability. Teachers' values appear to be one such important source.

As balance is an important theme in this book, I should point out that in writing it I myself have tried to strike a balance between a presentation and writing style that an elementary- or secondary-school teacher might find accessible but one that professional researchers and academics might also find acceptable. The risk, of course, is that I have not been able to satisfy either.

Nonetheless, the effort is worth making. The value of stability that teachers add in democratic societies today is important but it has, in the United States at least, received too little attention, mainly because of preoccupation with value-added teacher assessment. One purpose of the present work is to correct this imbalance by using data to suggest that the value teachers add to students' academic growth is no more important than the value they add to their moral development.

I should also say that the initial work on this project really began more than twenty years ago while I was a professor at the Louisiana State University where my friend and colleague Abbas Tashakkori and I first explored the idea of teachers as agents of change and keepers of tradition. At that time, however, there was not much data available and we shelved the idea for later. Life intervened thereafter, and we both went to different institutions and in different directions. But I am nonetheless grateful to Abbas for his continued friendship and the early collaboration that planted the seeds of this research.

I need also to mention my former student and now colleague Lauren Menard, who read portions of the manuscript and gave me very helpful feedback. Frank del Falvero also made a number of observations for which I am grateful and that helped me improve the work. Richard Fossey examined portions of the work with his critical eye and helped me make it better. Thanks as well to Dr. Nancy Autin for her careful readings and comments. I want also to say that I have been fortunate to have an excellent publishing team at Rowman & Littlefield, Tom Koerner, Caitlin Crawford, and Melissa McNitt who helped make this book better. Any weaknesses that may remain are, of course, my own doing.

I am grateful, as well, to my wife, Maria, for her support and encouragement during the writing of the manuscript. Finally, to my children, Sebastian, Alex, Thomas, and Dorothy to whom this work is dedicated, thank you. You are my constant joy, inspiration, and motivation.

NOTE

1. The Occupy Movement is, on its face, about inequality. But it is rooted in a virtually unlimited freedom to accumulate individual wealth. On the other hand, the argument for the right or freedom to own assault weapons with large magazines is grounded in a selfish desire to do pretty much whatever one wants without regard for the consequences for others.

Introduction

Whether we wish to admit it or not, every educational system tries to produce a certain kind of human being, and the tastes, sentiments, and dispositions it tries to develop in people depend upon the political system which it serves. Tyrannies, for example, need and want citizens who think, feel, and act in ways supportive of an authoritarian regime. The primary aim of education in such a society is not to teach people to think for themselves or question things as they are. It is rather to dispose them to be compliant and obedient.

Democracies, however, need lovers of equality and freedom, citizens who hold equality and freedom to be among their highest values, who keep a sharp lookout for threats to either, and who trust one another enough to overcome their individualism and unite their efforts when it becomes necessary to oppose threats to these two values.

While the values of equality and freedom function as central organizing principles for any democracy, in some democracies freedom is valued more than equality while in others the opposite is the case. In America, for historical and other reasons, freedom seems to be the *primus inter pares* or "the first among equals." Above all, it seems, Americans are lovers of freedom.

We should not be skeptical, therefore, if we find that American elementary- and secondary-school teachers tend to value freedom highly, probably even more highly than other Americans who do not teach for a living. They are, after all, explicitly charged with the task of passing on to the next generation our nation's founding principles and its history, not to mention more general values as well.

The country's attention these days is focused mainly on high-stakes tests and testing, and in the fog of the accountability movement, we tend to see only their impact on children's cognitive achievement and overlook their influence on the development of children's values. But whether we like it or not, teachers teach values, and in a democracy we can expect that freedom is one of the values they try hard to teach. And if this be so, then we can reasonably expect school teachers themselves to value freedom highly, perhaps even more than other Americans do.

Surprisingly, however, this is not the case. In fact, and as this study aims to show, some of the best data we have on Americans in general and teachers in particular indicate that American elementary and secondary teachers do not, as a group, tend to value freedom as highly as other Americans, particularly those with comparable levels of education. The question that naturally emerges from this finding is simply: Why? Why is it that American teachers are not as supportive of important aspects of freedom as other Americans?

The general conclusion—a hypothesis, really—of this book, and one that arises out of analyses of 40 years of data, is that school teachers tend to be less supportive than nonteachers of the value of freedom because individual freedom in America is being taken to extremes. Teachers are reacting to this excess and trying to curb or regulate it. Their effort to do so shows up in their values. They are less supportive of the value of freedom because they must deal every day with the reality of its excesses.

Through television, the Internet, and the entertainment industry, American culture encourages children to test the limits of individual liberty. The general message it sends them is that they are free to do and be pretty much anything they want. But usually left out of this message is the caveat that while they are free to experiment with self-expression, they ought not to do so without considering the consequences for others. The result, as Alexis de Tocqueville predicted, is that many children come to a radical individualist's understanding of freedom: freedom is being able to do whatever one wants without regard to its consequences for others.

Many children tend to carry this narrow understanding of freedom into the nation's classrooms, where teachers must deal with it. But teachers are faced with the task of managing not one but many children in a single room, often all day long, and they are also under increasing pressures to prepare their students to pass high-stakes accountability tests. They do not have the leisure, therefore, to allow their students to experiment with self-expression. Accordingly, they discourage children from testing the boundaries of freedom and thereby teach them that individual liberty, for all of its virtues and the pleasure it brings, has limits.

In teaching children the limits of liberty teachers, moreover, make an important but largely unacknowledged contribution to democracy in America: they help stabilize its unsteadiness.

That modern democracies are prone to be unsteady is not only a long-standing theme in the democracy literature but has also been readily observable to anyone who has paid attention over the last two decades to the vicissitudes of democracy around the globe.[1]

By the 1990s, democracy appeared to be on the march throughout the world. So rapidly were countries democratizing that some scholars, picking up on an Hegelian theme, wondered whether we had finally reached the "end of history," meaning that the long evolution of ways of ruling had at last reached a stage where the general model of government that had finally evolved—democracy—could be improved upon but not replaced by a better model.[2]

Within a generation, however, the fortunes of democracy appeared to be more uncertain. In 2010, for example, Freedom House reported that "for the fifth consecutive year, declines have trumped gains," and went on to say that the de-democratization process that seemed to be taking hold around the world represented ". . . the longest continuous period of deterioration in the nearly 40-year "history of Freedom House's annual assessment of the state of political and civil liberties in every country of the world."[3] Most recently, the 2013 report noted that "while the number of countries ranked as Free in 2012 was 90, a gain of 3 over the previous year, 27 countries showed significant declines than gains worldwide." As Bruce Gilley observed, "The hottest books on democratization . . . concern not democratic advance but authoritarian resurgence."[4]

In recent years, even confidence in the steadiness of democracy in the United States, always more or less taken for granted, has been shaken by an economic crisis and political gridlock. The United States began as a great experiment—and remains so today—in how to balance the vicissitudes of modern democracy with traditional values. Science and religion, reason and authority, self-expression and conformity, coordination and cooperation, freedom and order, equality and natural ability—these and dozens of other modern and postmodern tensions must be managed if America is not only to compete in the world but also to survive with the best of its founding principles intact. The values of its school teachers play no small role in whether Americans learn to manage these tensions well or poorly.

Teachers' contribution to the stabilization of democracy does not end, however, with their regulation of children's understanding of freedom. While they dampen or discourage excesses of freedom they are at the same time nurturing and encouraging other values, particularly those that support community and the development of social capital—the so-called "social virtues."[5] In the case of these values, the data suggest that teachers tend to be *more* supportive than other Americans. They tend to be so, we maintain, because modern advanced capitalist democracies tend to undermine these values and teachers serve to counteract this corrosive tendency.

This is the case, at least, for the value of trust which, as Robert Putnam and others have found, has been on the decline in America, and probably in other modern democracies as well.[6] Teachers tend to be more trusting than other Americans, particularly more so than those having only a high-school education or less. The first contacts that many of America's children probably have of adults with high levels of trust, therefore, may well occur in the schools where they encounter and work with teachers.

It also happens to be the case for values such as helpfulness, cooperativeness, fairness, and the like. As a group, teachers tend, more than others, to have an optimistic view of human nature, to see people as being basically helpful and fair as opposed to being noncooperative, only out for themselves, and disposed to take advantage. Here, too, teachers are also likely to be many children's first encounter with adults who see more good than bad in people.

So, while teachers check the effects of some democratic values, such as freedom, they cultivate others, particularly the social values that underpin civil society and, through it, democracy. This seems to be the case in the United States, at any rate, and whether it is so in other democracies is a hypothesis that needs to be tested in further research.

Teachers have the impact they do on society in part because of the sheer size and reach of their occupation. In the United States, for example, there are approximately 3.7 million elementary- and secondary-school teachers, public and private, at work five days a week during the school year. America's teaching force is twice the size of its military and would fill more than 37 Rose Bowls. In its largest cities and smallest towns, in the farthest reaches of the land, one can find a school. Working within it are women and men who dedicate their lives to children's education and protection. Teaching is unique among modern occupations in that it reaches almost everyone. Few other occupations can claim its pervasiveness.

Rich or poor, no matter their color, intelligence, or levels of ambition, most people have worked closely and intensely with teachers, and for long periods and during impressionable stages of their lives. The impact teachers have is profound and lifelong. This is not only the case for America, but for every modern society. Most of us can still recall at least one or two of our elementary- or secondary-school teachers.

Teachers influenced not only what we came to know but also what we learned to value. Theirs was not only knowledge work but values work as well. When they taught us English, mathematics, science, or social studies, they also conveyed messages about the value of hard work, of doing things that we might not have liked, of perseverance, and so on. They served, too, as models of trust, cooperation, fairness, and the like. Perhaps not all of our teachers influenced us in positive ways, but for ill or good they influenced us nonetheless. Teachers made a difference in our lives and still do in the lives of our children.

Teachers' impact on our values, however, is not the priority in education today. In America, and in many other countries of the world as well, almost everything is focused on tests and testing. Teachers are being judged on how much they can increase students test scores from one year to the next. These year-to-year gains in scores are being referred to as "value added," and value-added teacher assessment is now all the rage. "Good" teachers are those who show they can add value, that is, raise test scores.

The main point of this book is that while teachers may add value when they enable students to increase their performance on standardized tests, this is not the only and not even the most important value they add. An equally if not more important value added is their contribution to the stabilization of unsteady democracy. We need not only to recognize this fact but also to avoid policies that tend to undermine their capacity to carry out this vital function, a function upon which democracy in America and elsewhere in the world no little depends.[7]

ORGANIZATION OF THE BOOK

The analyses out of which this conclusion emerges begins in chapter 1 with some general observations on teachers and the teaching profession in the United States. Its aim is to alert the reader to the fact that teachers not only teach mathematics, science, reading, social studies, and other subjects, but they also teach values. They do so as much indirectly as directly, by *how* they teach these traditional subjects and the ways they comport themselves as they are teaching. Included here as well are demographic facts about the teachers and their profession of which most readers may be aware but only in the most general terms.

As this book is about the values of teachers, some attention needs to be paid to what values are and how they function in society, and this is the aim of chapter 2 on values and valuing. In this chapter, two main themes are discussed. One has to do with the research done by the World Values Association. This research suggests that at the center of all societies' value systems lie two important values tensions: order versus freedom, and faith versus reason. Many other values relationships appear to be linked to these two values pairs.

The second theme has to do with a theory about the role that values play in a democracy, a theory espoused by two twentieth-century thinkers: the sociologist Max Weber and the political philosopher Allan Bloom. At the core of this theory is the idea that in advanced democracies in general and in democracy in America in particular, the tension between faith and reason plays out such that politics may become irrational and democracy self-destructive. Leadership is needed to counteract this self-destructive tendency.

Following the discussion of teachers and values in chapters 1 and 2, chapters 3 through 8 turn to an examination of data on specific values. Chapter 3 focuses on the oft-mentioned "family values." National data on marriage, divorce, abortion, and homosexuality are examined here. Also discussed is how much importance Americans in general and teachers in particular attach to five values commonly felt to be important for children to learn. Americans' views on these values are then compared to those held by peoples of 57 other nations.

Chapter 4 deals with religion and religious values. Teachers, as it turns out, tend to be more religious than nonteachers, and this affects their views of a number of other values.

Chapter 5 concerns the social values, also sometimes referred to as the "social virtues." These are the values that enable people to come together voluntarily to solve common problems and engage in common endeavors. Here the key values discussed are "trust," "helpfulness," and "fairness," values that are believed to be necessary for social capital formation and the maintenance of civil society, the latter considered to be the foundation of a healthy democracy.

Chapters 6 and 7 deal with two values that are considered most central to a democracy: equality and freedom. Chapter 8 deals with teachers' knowledge of and, by implication, their appreciation for science.

Chapter 9 concludes with an essay on the role of teachers' values in a democratic society, given the latter's propensity to be unsteady.

NOTES

1. See, for example, Fareed Zacharia, "The Rise of Illiberal Democracy," *Foreign Affairs* 76 (1997): 22–43.

2. Francis Fukuyama, *The End of History and the Last Man* (New York: Free Press, 1992).

3. Freedom House, "Freedom in the World: 2010–2013," www.freedom-house.org/template.cfm2page=15.

4. Bruce Gilley, "Democratic Triumph, Scholarly Pessimism," *Journal of Democracy* 21 (2010): 161. See also Robert Slater, "Developmental Democracy, Accountability and Educational Leadership," *International Journal of Leadership in Education* 15 (2012): 387–94.

5. See Francis Fukuyama, *Trust: The Social Virtues and the Creation of Prosperity* (New York: Free Press, 1995), 5.

6. Robert Putnam, *Bowling Alone: The Collapse and Revival of American Community* (New York: Simon & Schuster, 2000).

7. For a detailed discussion of education policies that threaten to undermine traditional democratic values, see Diane Ravitch, *The Death and Life of the Great American School System* (New York: Basic Books, 2010).

Part I

TEACHERS,
TEACHING, AND VALUES

Chapter One

Teachers and Teaching

Teaching not only conveys ideas, it also shapes values. As it brings about children's intellectual development, it stimulates their moral development as well. Teachers not only teach our children how to think and solve problems. They also help form their beliefs about what is right, good, and important in life, shaping their values in the process.

In liberal-democratic societies there is always a desire to separate the teaching of values from the teaching of reading, writing, and mathematics, the so-called value-neutral subjects. But what every parent who has done homework with his child knows is that, like it or not, we teach values in the course of teaching these value-neutral subjects. We teach, for example, the values of hard work, of doing things that we may not like, of persevering in the face of difficulty, of listening to and respecting the efforts of adults, of self-initiated effort, of postponement of gratification, of meeting deadlines, and the like. All of these simple lessons are moral lessons, lessons about what is important, and about what ought to be taken seriously.

So even when teachers try to be value-neutral, their teaching—by the manner in which they do it and the nature of their interactions in the course of it—conveys messages to children about how they should regard themselves, consider others, and meet their obligations. Teaching is a moral effort as well as an intellectual enterprise, and teachers influence not only what our children come to know but what they come to believe and value as well.

In the Fall of 2012, over 55 million schoolchildren attended elementary and secondary schools, both private and public, in the United States, a number that exceeds the populations of Spain and Sweden combined.

From August through May, these students spent about 180 days in school, at least six hours a day, for a total of about 1,040 hours.[1,2]

To appreciate just how much time this is, we need only keep in mind that, on average, American schoolchildren spend less than three hours per day engaged with their parents in activities that can in anyway compare with the intensity of schooling.[3] Even if we assume that children are doing meaningful things with their parents for three hours a day, 365 days a year, we still come up with a total not much greater than the amount of time that these same children spend in school. Of the two social institutions—family and school—perhaps the family does have a more profound impact on our children's development. But the effects of school cannot be far behind. Next to family life, life in schools is the most intense and sustained that our children have.[4]

The considerable time that America's elementary- and secondary-school students spend in school is mainly spent with teachers, and what teachers do with our children during this time not only stands to make them more or less learned but also to make them better or worse human beings.

In light of the moral impact that teachers have on our children, it would seem useful to know something about their own values. What are the values of America's elementary- and secondary-school teachers? As a group, what do they hold dear and deem to be most important? Moreover, do their values and value structure significantly differ from those of other Americans who are not engaged in teaching as their profession? What do our teachers believe, for example, about the things a democratic society holds or should hold to be most important? What do they believe about freedom, equality, and trust? Where do they stand, as well, on the most controversial moral issues of our time—God, religion, family, sexuality, marriage, and the like?

The short answer to these questions is that we simply do not know, though we have a natural tendency to think that we do. Teaching is one of the most visible occupations in our social structure. Few of us have occasion to interact with mining engineers, archivists, brick masons, or derrick men. But almost all of us have dealt and deal with teachers.

Our postindustrial societies are rapidly morphing into knowledge societies, and in knowledge societies teachers are everywhere. As a result, they are familiar to us all and most of us feel we know something about them and their craft. But this, like so many other things in social life, is a convenient illusion. We think we know what in fact we only assume.

To be sure, there has been a good deal of quality research and knowledge generated about teachers in the context of teaching, on teachers and their lives and work in schools, two classic examples of which are Willard Waller's *The Sociology of Teaching* and Dan Lortie's *Schoolteacher.*[5] But when it comes to their lives outside of education—especially their general beliefs and values—we actually know relatively little about them. One goal of this study is to help fill this gap.

Much of the data in this study comes from two sources. One is the National Opinion Research Center's General Social Survey, one of the largest, most reliable, and frequently used data sets in the social sciences. The version used here is the one made conveniently available online by the Computer-Assisted Survey Methods Program at the University of California–Berkeley.[6] Readers who have access to the Internet can easily check for themselves the analysis and the tables from which the propositions in this study are derived and upon which they are based. Another source of data is the World Values Survey, and this as well is made conveniently online for those who wish to check the analysis herein.[7]

The data are good and reliable but we need, at the outset, to be clear about the limitations of this study. In the first place, it is a preliminary survey, a first reconnoitering from afar, as it were, of an intellectual territory not previously seen from the distance provided herein. Accordingly, many important details simply remain indistinct, details that will need to be observed before it can be said that we have anything like an understanding of teachers' values. Understanding, in this sense of the term, can only be approached by more qualitative research of the type outlined in Denzin and Lincoln's useful and already classic compendium.[8] Another objective of this study is to provide such qualitative researchers some clues about what to look for in future qualitative work on teachers' values.

While it might not result in the kind of knowledge that only qualitative investigation can provide, this study is not without its uses. Before we can presume to understand a thing we must first be aware of its existence. If this study does little more than increase the general awareness of teachers' values and the impact that advanced democratic societies have on them, it will not have been effort wasted.

A second limitation of the study is that it does not differentiate between public- and private-school teachers. Approximately 11 percent of the 3.7 million elementary- and secondary-school teachers in this country work in private schools. Accordingly, the different work settings are likely to emphasize some values over others. Religious values, for example, may be more prominent among teachers who work in private schools affiliated with churches than in public schools.

In Catholic schools, for example, religious values are a key component of the curriculum, and Catholic-school teachers may be more likely to express, if not hold, religious values whereas teachers in public schools, while they may privately hold religious beliefs, are not supposed to make these part of the curriculum and therefore may be less apt to express them in interviews. So, if we find that teachers in general tend to be more religious than nonteachers, it may well be because we have in our sample a percentage of teachers who work in private, religiously affiliated schools. Our data do not efficiently allow us to differentiate between private-school teachers and their public-school counterparts. Nonetheless, as already noted, private-school teachers make up only 11 percent of the U.S. teaching force. Moreover, throughout the analysis we do control for religiousness as measured by church attendance. Accordingly, some control has been put on the effects of religion.

There is nothing new about the idea that teachers' work bestows upon those who do it a particular social image and, by implication, a particular self-image with a correlated value structure. Willard Waller devotes considerable attention to the notion, and teacher stereotypes have been common not only in popular culture ("Welcome back Kotter," *Educating Rita, Dead Poets' Society*) but in Shakespeare as well.[9] It is not far-fetched, then, to suppose that an occupation that lends itself so readily to the formation of special social images and ideals does not also bestow upon, or at least attract, practitioners who tend to see the world and the human condition in ways that differ from how most others see them, or who deem things to be more or less important or take them more or less seriously than do others occupied in different lines of work. There seems to be sufficient intellectual precedent, then, to justify an empirical examination of whether, how and even why the values of American teachers might differ from the values of Americans in general.

In comparing teachers' values with those of nonteachers', we can also gain some perspective on America's central value tendencies. Values, the beliefs we deem important and live by, are things that not only give individual lives integrity but give societies their integrity as well; these are part of the social glue that helps keep things from falling apart. Imagine a society has having a moral "center" and "periphery" with its core values lying at its center and increasingly less mainstream values as we move from its center to its periphery, where we find values held by only a small percent of the population.[10] With this imagery, teachers' values are most likely to be at the center. This is because teachers and teaching have as one of their major functions the transmission of values from one generation to the next. Societies depend on their teachers, their elementary- and secondary-school teachers especially, to maintain their integrity across generations. So, in studying teachers' values we are also gaining a window onto America's values, and are able to see how and to what degree they may deviate from those of teachers. Thus, a study of teachers' values is at the same time a study of America's core values.

Before moving to our examination of teachers' values, however, it might be useful to get some introductory knowledge of their demographics. To this we next turn.

SELECTED DEMOGRAPHIC CHARACTERISTICS

We should begin by noting a few things about the occupation of teaching, especially as it compares in some fundamental ways with other occupations in the United States. Perhaps most important, and as we have already noted, is its sheer size. There are an estimated 3.7 million public and private elementary- and secondary-school teachers in the United States.[11] The K–12 teaching occupation is one of the largest occupations in America. There are more teachers in America than cashiers (3.3 million), and more than twice the number in the military, which has about 1.4 men and women in uniform.[12]

The enormous size of the teaching occupation holds important practical implications. Among these is the problem of recruiting new members. Unlike the smaller occupations for which we can pick and choose among the top candidates, the occupation of teaching requires us to delve deep into the pool of prospective teachers to fill its ranks. This necessity is made even more pressing in light of the teacher-turnover statistics. In the 2008–2009 school year, 8 percent of America's public-school teachers left the profession and 16 percent of its private-school teachers did so. The combined total of leavers was 347,000.[13] As a result of this kind of turnover, over half of America's teachers quit teaching within five years of entering the occupation, a fact that causes school systems across the country to have to scramble continually for new recruits. As a result, school officials often have to reach deep into the teaching pool to get the teachers they need, and the basic educational background of teachers tends to range more broadly than does that of the other professions and semi-professions.

We can see this, for example, on the results of a simple vocabulary test. At one point in the survey interview from which much of the data for this study are derived, the field worker gives the respondent a vocabulary test. The test consists of ten words. For each of the ten words there are five other words, one of which most closely matches the meaning of the vocabulary word. The respondent is asked to choose the correct match for each of the ten vocabulary words. Now, in 2012, only a little more than one-third of all Americans surveyed got seven to 10 of the answers correct. But two-thirds of American elementary and secondary teachers got this many correct.

Not surprisingly, and perhaps contrary to what some cynics of American education might expect, our teachers tend to do much better on this test than nonteachers do. Teachers do not, however, do as well when compared with better-educated Americans, with, say, medical doctors and lawyers. In this case, 88 percent of the physicians and lawyers get seven or more correct while, again, only two-thirds of the teachers do.

We should not make too much of these data, but they do suggest that doctors and lawyers have stronger educational backgrounds. This may be the case simply because their professions can be and are more selective in the recruitment process. There are about 660,000 physicians in the United States and about 840,000 lawyers.[14] The medical and law professions do not, therefore, have to delve as deeply into the national pool of educated labor as the teaching profession does with its 3.7 million members. They can be and are more selective in their admissions policies. The size of the teaching occupation, on the other hand, requires consideration of applicants at lower levels of educational preparation.

THE HOMOGENEITY OF THE TEACHING FORCE

In a group with this many individuals one would expect to find considerable diversity. But the teaching profession is surprisingly homogeneous. In some respects it is more so than the general population. For example, most of the elementary- and secondary-school teachers in this country are women, about 75 percent over all.[15] Most are white; only about 7 percent of America's elementary- and secondary-school teachers are African American, while about 13 percent of the U.S. population as a whole is, and about 16 percent of their students are.[16] Most American elementary- and secondary-school teachers are in their 40s, their median age being 46. If we examine the data from the most recent decade, we find that about 68 percent of them are married as compared to about 55 percent for the general population. About 6 percent are widowed, the same as other Americans. The percentage of teachers divorced during the last decade (about 8 percent) is slightly smaller than that of nonteachers for the same period. About one-quarter of American teachers do not have children and the other three-fourths that do, tend to have two. On average, our teachers have been teaching for about 14 years. Like most other Americans, they tend to work hard, typically putting in 50-hour work weeks. For this effort, elementary- and secondary-school teachers averaged a little over $56,000 a year in 2010–2011. Their incomes exceeded the average for Americans generally which was $41,671, but was about equal to the average for Americans with bachelor's degrees.[17] About 60 percent seem to be satisfied with their work as they say they would either certainly or probably be willing to teach again.

What diversity one does find in the teaching cadre appears to be developing slowly, and mirrors the general trend in the population as a whole. For example, the percent of Americans who said they were U.S.-born has decreased by about 6 percentage points over the past four decades, going from about 93 percent in the 1970s to about 87 percent in the 2000s—a little more than a 6 percent decline. Similarly, the percent of American teachers who said they were U.S. born has gone from 98 percent to about 91—a 7 percent decline.

So, while the size of the occupation alone would lead one to expect considerable diversity among elementary- and secondary-school teachers in the United States, this is not the case. Teachers as a group show a remarkable degree of homogeneity. They are mostly white, middle-aged females who have been teaching for about 14 years, are married with two children, and have annual earnings close to the median earnings of college-educated Americans.

POINTS TO REMEMBER

- The purpose of this book is to address the following questions: What are the values of America's elementary- and secondary-school teachers? As a group, what do they hold dear and deem to be most important? Moreover, do their values differ from those of other Americans who are not engaged in teaching as their profession? What do our teachers believe, for example, about the things a democratic society holds or should hold to be most important? What do they believe about freedom, equality, and trust? Where do they stand, as well, on the most controversial moral issues of our time—God, religion, family, sexuality, marriage, and the like?
- We should want to know about teachers' values because their values influence children's values. Whether they realize it or not, teachers teach values while they develop children's cognitive capacities.
- By studying teachers' values we can also learn something about ourselves as a country and as a culture, because teachers work at the center of a society's value system.
- Teachers teach values by *how* they teach, how they treat others, and by what they say and how they comport themselves in children's presence.
- We know a good deal about teachers in the context of their work but we know much less about their general values, especially those values that are felt to be important for children to acquire if they are to live well in and contribute to a democratic society.
- In modern societies, teaching is one of the largest occupations. There are approximately 3.7 million elementary- and secondary-school teachers in the United States, a number that is twice the size of its military.

• The size of the American teaching force notwithstanding, the occupation of teaching is surprisingly homogeneous. Three-quarters of elementary- and secondary-school teachers are women, most are white, in their mid-40s, and are married with children of their own.

NOTES

1. U.S. Department of Education, National Center for Education Statistics, 2011, nces.ed.gov/fastfacts/display.asp?id=65.

2. Institute for Education Sciences, National Center for Education Statistics, 2008, nces.ed.gov/programs/digest/d08/tables/dt08_166.asp.

3. Anne Gauthier, Timothy Smeeding, and Frank Furstenberg, Jr., "Are Parents Investing Less Time in Children? Trends in Selected Industrialized Countries," *Population and Development Review* 30 (December 2004): 647–71.

4. For a classic description of life in schools, see Phillip Jackson's *Life in Classrooms* (New York: Teachers College Press, 1968).

5. See Willard Waller, *The Sociology of Teaching* (New York: Wiley, 1932), and Dan C. Lortie's *Schoolteacher* (Chicago: The University of Chicago Press, 1975). For more recent work, see Virginia Richardson, ed., *Handbook of Research on Teaching*, rev. ed. (Washington, DC: American Educational Research Association, 2001), and Andy Hargreaves, *Teaching in the Knowledge Society: Education in the Age of Insecurity* (New York: Teachers' College Press and Buckingham, UK: Open University Press, 2003).

6. University of California–Berkeley, Computer-Assisted Survey Methods Program: The GSS Cumulative Data File 1972–2010, 2011, sda.berkeley.edu/index.html.

7. "World Values Survey," World Values Survey Association, www.worldvaluessurvey.org/.

8. Norman Denzin and Yvonna Lincoln, eds., *The Sage Handbook of Qualitative Research*, 3rd ed. (Thousand Oaks, CA: Sage Publications, 2005).

9. See David Greenblatt's engaging *Will in the World: How Shakespeare Became Shakespeare* (New York: Norton, 2005).

10. On this point see Edward Shils, *Center and Periphery* (Chicago: University of Chicago Press, 1975).

11. See U.S. Department of Education, National Center for Education Statistics (2012), Digest of Education Statistics, 2011 (NCES 2012-001), Introduction and chap. 2; U.S. Department of Education, National Center for Education Statistics, Schools and Staffing Survey, Teacher Data Files, 2007–08, nces.ed.gov/

fastfacts/display.asp?id=28 and Bureau of Labor Statistics, *Occupational Employment and Wages News Release* (2011), www.bls.gov/news.release/ocwage. htm.

12. U.S. Department of Defense, *Military Personnel Strength Figures* (2011), kb.defense.gov/app/answers/detail/a_id/253/session/L3RpbWUvMTMyMzI2OT kwMy9zaWQvdTVPNCotS2s%3D.

13. Institute of Education Science, National Center for Education Statistics, "Teacher Turnover: Stayers, Leavers and Movers (Indicator 32-2011), nces. ed.gov/programs/coe/indicator_tat.asp. In addition, only a little over 100,000 K–12 teachers receive bachelor's degrees in education each year from all of the country's postsecondary institutions combined, not enough to replace those who are leaving. For these figures and others, see S. Aud, W. Hussar, G. Kena, K. Bianco, L. Frohlich, J. Kemp, and K. Tahan, "Indicator 40: Undergraduate Fields of Study," U.S. Department of Education, National Center for Education Statistics, Washington, DC: U.S. Government Printing Office, nces.ed.gov/programs/ coe/indicator_fsu.asp, and Gillian Hampden-Thompson, William L. Herring, and Gregory Kienzl, "Issue Brief: Attrition of Public School Mathematics and Science Teachers," Institute of Education Sciences, U.S. Department of Education: Washington, DC: U.S. Government Printing Office.

14. Bureau of Labor Statistics, *May 2010 National Occupational Employment and Wage Estimates United States* (2010), www.bls.gov/oes/current/oes_nat. htm#29-0000.

15. National Center for Education Statistics, Digest of Education Statistics: 2010, "Highest Degree Earned and Years of Full-Time Teaching Experience for Teachers in Public and Private Secondary Schools, by Selected Teacher Characteristics:1999–2000, 2003–04, and 2007–2008," nces.ed.gov/programs/digest/ d10/tables/dt10_072.asp?referrer=report.

16. U.S. Department of Education, National Center for Education Statistics (2012), Digest of Education Statistics, 2011 (NCES 2012-001), Introduction and chap. 2; U.S. Department of Education, National Center for Education Statistics, Schools and Staffing Survey, Teacher Data Files, 2007–08, nces.ed.gov/fastfacts/ display.asp?id=28.

17. National Center for Education Statistics. (2012). Fast Facts. http://nces. ed.gov/fastfacts/display.asp?id=28, and U.S. Department of Labor, Bureau of Labor Statistics (2012). "Earnings and Unemployment Rates by Educational Attainment" http://www.bls.gov/emp/ep_chart_001.htm.

Chapter Two

Values and Valuing

Values are to human beings what instincts are to animals; they guide our behavior. We use the word "guide" advisedly, of course, understanding that instinct is not, by definition, reflective while values precisely are, a feature that makes them one of the characteristics that differentiates humans from other animals.

Human beings are the "esteeming" beings, said Nietzsche, the beasts with "red cheeks." But he could have just as well said that we are the "valuing" beings, for to expect admiration and respect—honor—from others, and to be embarrassed when we fail to receive it is a form of valuation; we value or hold high the opinions of others and are ashamed when we fail to live up to them. Values and valuing are among the defining elements of the human condition.

Psychologists define values as "conceptions of the desirable," that influence our judgments, decisions, and actions.[1] By this definition, values consist of two major components: conceptualization and desire or, what amounts to the same thing, reason and desire.

The term "conceptions" in this definition indicates the rational aspect of values, the role that conceptualization or reason must play when we engage in the act of valuing. The term "desirable" stresses the emotional aspect. Values, by this definition, then, are neither wholly rational nor completely emotional but are combinations of reason and emotion or, as the values psychologists prefer, desire.[2]

The problem of the relationship between reason and desire has occupied thinkers from the earliest beginnings of philosophy and literature, and still occupies us today. That it does so is evidenced by academic books like Howard Gardner's work on multiple intelligences and, on the

21

more popular side, by Daniel Goldman's book on emotional intelligence.[3] Both of these works, as well as others lesser known, may be viewed as efforts to correct our inclination to see the world in terms of opposites—cognitive versus social development, reason versus emotion, self versus other, and so on.

The approach we shall take here is to view these various pairs of opposites as extremes on a continuum. In each case of opposites, it is not so much a question of either/or but rather what the balance between the opposites actually is, and what it should be and why it should be so.

This approach is consistent with that taken by many values researchers who, rather than thinking about values in terms of either/or, prefer instead to see them as lying along various continua.

In fact, researchers involved in the World Values Survey (WVS), an ongoing international research project on values in more than 50 countries, argue that much of the data on values can be organized with the aid of two pairs of values.[4] On the one hand, nations can be ranked according to whether their populations tend to be religious or secular in orientation. On the other, they can also be differentiated according to whether people are more concerned with security or with self-expression. The religious—secular pair of values, as well as the security—self-expression pair, are both viewed as extremes on a continuum and not as simple either/or phenomena.

The discovery by the WVS researchers that many human values can be understood in terms of the religion—secularism and the security—self-expression coordinates can also help us to understand the values of American school teachers. The values of American school teachers tend to be progressive when compared to the U.S. population as a whole, but at the same time, they are often more conservative than highly educated Americans, that is, those with bachelor's degrees and higher. This, for example, is the case with the value of freedom. Teachers tend to be more supportive of freedom than the general population but less so than comparably educated Americans.

At the same time, however, teachers tend to support some values more so than anyone else. This is the case, for example, with the value of trust. Teachers tend to be more trusting than other Americans regardless of their education, gender, race, class, or religious commitment.

TEACHER VALUES AND DEMOCRACY IN AMERICA

Education, as we shall see, has a powerful liberalizing effect, and so it is not surprising that teachers tend to be more liberal than Americans with less education than they have, for most teachers have university degrees. What is surprising, however, is that teachers are more conservative than American nonteachers who also hold university degrees.

We would expect teachers and the most highly educated Americans to be equally liberal. But they are not. Teachers are often more conservative than Americans who are comparably educated, and this difference does not appear to be a result of their age, gender, income, race, class, religiousness, or region of the country in which they work. So, what is behind this teacher conservatism?

Now, at the same time, just as teachers tend to be more conservative than comparably educated Americans on some important values, such as freedom, they also happen to be more progressive on others. In this case the values involved are the so-called "social virtues," values such as cooperativeness, fairness, trust, and the like.[5] But again, the question that arises is why should teachers' values not be the same?

Some of the explanation for teacher conservatism may have to do with the nature of their occupations, as Dan Lortie maintained in *Schoolteacher*. But their occupational characteristics would not seem to account for their simultaneous progressivism. Our position is that in addition to occupational influences, other, broader factors are at work as well.

A central hypothesis advanced in this book is that teacher conservatism and progressivism are in no small part responses to the nature and condition of democracy in America. Teacher conservatism and progressivism, it will be suggested, are in part a response to a democracy threatened by two self-destructive imbalances:

1. a wide-spread understanding of freedom as being free to do whatever one wants, often regardless of the consequences for others, and
2. a tendency for people, when trying to understand themselves, to think only of the opinions of others, and when dealing with others, to think only of themselves. The values of American teachers work to counteract both of these tendencies. Their conservatism is largely a response

to the first, and their progressivism is mainly a reaction to the second. This, at least, is the hypothesis that emerges from the analysis to follow.

Before turning to this analysis, however, we should mention Larry Cuban's recent finding that teachers tend to teach in ways that "hug the middle," for this finding bears on ours as well.

Cuban says that teachers tend to balance "teacher-centered" with "student-centered" pedagogy. The former tends to ignore diversity in the classroom while the latter tries to accommodate instruction to individual student differences and learning styles. Teachers' efforts to balance the two instructional approaches have been complicated, he says, by our nation's current obsession with high-stakes testing and accountability—a complication, by the way, that is likely to be made more so by the recent development of "value-added" teacher assessments.

An historical note may help clarify this point for noneducators. Since the publication of "A Nation at Risk" during the Reagan administration, pressures to centralize American education have accelerated. One of the key strategies for doing this has been the development of high-stakes tests and, more recently, a national curriculum.

At the same time, however, and mainly in the interest of diversity, teachers have been taught to move away from traditional, teacher-centered approaches to teaching, wherein their instructional decisions tended, as we have already noted, to ignore student diversity and individual learning styles, and toward a more student-centered approach whereby individual differences are accommodated. The problem is that the kind of instruction that seems most effective in preparing students to pass high-stakes tests tends to be teacher-centered, while the demands of diversity require a more student-centered approach. Teachers, faced with pressures for both, try to do both but as the stakes or so high, they tend to err, as it were, on the side of the tests.

Cuban's teachers-hug-the-middle thesis is important for our purposes because it makes sense in terms of the broader issues we introduce in the next section, and once these broader forces are understood, it will also serve as a basis for predicting what might happen to teachers' values in the future.

More will be said on this point in due course but at this juncture it is sufficient to note that if Cuban is correct about teachers' hugging the middle, they are likely, simply out of the necessity of protecting their jobs, to become more conservative in their pedagogy, a point about which Cuban is well aware. But what the analysis to follow will further suggest is that the current conservatism–progressivism balance reflected in our teachers' values holds implications that go well beyond our classrooms and schools, and have to do with the nature and condition of American democracy itself. If we continue to carry our educational reforms to extremes, we stand to disrupt this imbalance with consequences that go beyond education.

Teachers are human beings, of course, and by no means perfect, and their adulation is certainly not the intention of the present work. Indeed, as we will show, in some respects—their knowledge of science being one—too many of them demonstrate a level of weakness that is not only worrisome but calls for urgent correction.

As a group, however, our teachers are among our democracy's greatest benefactors. They serve to check our natural tendency to leap into change before we look, and they serve as well as critical reservoirs of trust, helpfulness, cooperation, and fairness. Without our teachers' values to temper our excesses and to counteract our tendencies toward dissolution, our children would not only suffer badly, but democracy in America would itself be more at risk. In the next section, we will briefly try to suggest why this is so.

THE VALUES AND
VICISSITUDES OF MODERN DEMOCRACY

Among the things that American presidential campaigns make clear—and the 2012 campaign was no exception—is that the values debate is alive and well in America. But what exactly is this debate about, and why does talk about values persist in our culture, even in nonelection years, albeit in muted form? Why do we feel so compelled to talk about values?

One theory is that we talk about values so much because we moderns have tried to use them as substitutes for religion with its language of good and evil, and as such they are proving to be both too little and too much for us. We are finding them to be too little because they are but pale substitutes for religion. Unlike good and evil, values are not powerful enough to allow us to orient and anchor ourselves, especially in the face of the gale-force winds of nihilism and anomie—modern democracy's dark sides—that have battered the West in general and America in particular.

Values are proving to be too much for us, on the other hand, because they have tended to become more and more devoid of the reason and reasonableness that make them values in the first place, two recent and notable examples being gun control and federal budget politics.

This theory can be found both implicit and explicit in the works of two modern thinkers: Max Weber, the German sociologist perhaps best known for his *The Protestant Ethic and the Spirit of Capitalism*, and Allan Bloom, the controversial American political philosophy professor and author of *The Closing of the American Mind*, now a quarter of century old.[6]

As a culture, these two scholars suggest, the United States tried to jettison the belief in good and evil when, to use Friedrich Nietzsche's phrase, it tried to get "beyond good and evil," get past religion, which the modern mind views as at best inconvenient and at worst dangerous. Many Americans may have even thought that we had gotten past it. But as Bloom put it, and as recent politics suggest, "Enlightenment killed God but like Macbeth, the men of Enlightenment did not know that the cosmos would rebel at the deed."

Weber said that the ultimate outcome of the secularization or rationalization of Western societies would be a fragmentation of values into either/or choices that would admit of no compromise, compromise being the sine qua non of democracy.

Democracies, as Bloom noted, are the "regimes of reason," the rational regimes whose presidents cannot, as the kings of old, simply lop off the heads (at least not literally) of those who disagree with them. Values, by this view, are the rational regimes substitutes for good and evil. Values, like good and evil, are beliefs. But they differ from good and evil in the measure of their ingredients. While the recipe for good and evil calls for more emotion than reason, that for values calls for more reason than emotion.

This is not to say that emotion plays no role in values. On the contrary, when we value a thing we are not neutral about it. We have strong feelings. But the emotions or feelings we have with regard to them do not, at least in a functionally healthy democracy, rise to the intensity of the emotions and feelings involved in perceiving the world in terms of good and evil. Reason is supposed to reign in a democracy and when it does, the balance between reason and emotion is skewed toward reason in most things and especially in politics.

Whether or not values function as they should, however, and serve as rational-emotional guides and motives for our actions, depends in no small way on just how rational the rational regime is. Values, after all, exist in a context and that context is democracy. The condition of the democracy itself influences how well its values and value structure functions. When reason and common sense reign in a democracy, values do their job. However, when democracy grows irrational, so also do values as they tend to revert back to their old-time-religion mode.

Why and how democracies can grow irrational, becoming "illiberal," to use Fareed Zakaria's description, is a question too large to explore here in its general form. Democracy can be lost in different ways. No little depends on the particular history of the democracy in question.

Alexis de Tocqueville suggests that democracy has a latent tendency to become imbalanced, to go to extremes of various sorts. On this view, perhaps the root of the problems with democracy in America today has to do with the imbalance between freedom and equality. This makes sense not only in terms of current events, most notably the Occupy Movement, but also in light of our history. As Harvard historian Bernard Bailyn has observed, America was founded on paranoia about freedom. If we have erred on the side of freedom at the expense of equality it is perhaps understandable in view of our history, though nonetheless an imbalance in need of redress.

Tocqueville also reminds us that "democracy" is not simply a political arrangement but an economic one as well. Though he did not use the term, when he writes of democracy he means "capitalist" democracy. This meaning is suggested when he says, "Democratic institutions awaken and flatter the passion for equality without ever being able to satisfy it entirely . . . [people] are excited by the chance and irritated by the uncertainty of success; their excitement is followed by weariness and then by bitterness."

Our preoccupation with values, then, appears rooted in a bigger issue, namely, the condition of democracy in America. Teachers, especially, must be sensitive to this condition and their values can be expected to reflect it.

Teachers' values should somehow reflect the condition of our society simply because they must work with our children almost every day, and our children reflect the values of their parents and their communities—our society. They cannot help but carry these values into the schools and classrooms of America.

So, where our society exposes our children to models and lessons of indiscriminate freedom and self-expression—whether in the form of video games or other means—and creates in them a disposition to go to extremes, our teachers, simply out of the necessity to carry on an orderly instructional environment, must check and constrain them, teaching them in the process, an acceptable balance between self-expression or freedom and order and control. We should not be surprised, then, if our teachers tend to be more conservative where issues of freedom are concerned.

Nor should we be surprised if it turns out that our teachers demonstrate higher trust levels, and give a bit more importance than do nonteachers to the values of fairness, responsibility, caring, and the other "social virtues." Our society—most if not all modern societies, it seems—tends to erode the social virtues, and to the extent this is true, it is felt by our children who, again, carry the effects into our nation's classrooms and schools where our teachers must deal with and correct them.

POINTS TO REMEMBER

- Psychologists define values as "conceptions of the desirable." Values, therefore, must consist of our conceptions of what is true, good, or beautiful—all of which things we find desirable.
- Our values form a system of interconnected values, many of which are always in tension. Two important tensions or balances in the value systems of most societies are, first, the tension between order and security on the one hand and freedom and self-expression on the other, and, second, between faith and belief on the one side and secularism and reason on the other. These two tensions are central and influence each other as well as many other balances in a democratic society.
- Democratic societies tend to strike the balance between order and freedom on the side of freedom and self-expression. In some societies, such as the United States, there is, mainly for historical reasons, a marked tendency to take self-expression and freedom to extremes.

- The American tendency to take freedom and self-expression to excess is likely influenced by its general culture rooted in a unique combination of freedom and radical individualism. The general conception of the freedom component of its culture originated in what Harvard historian Bernard Bailyn described as a freedom infused with paranoia that dominated its revolutionary period. The U.S. culture's individualism component is influenced by what Alexis de Tocqueville described as "radical" individualism. This combination of radical individualism and freedom-born-of-strains-of-paranoia can and does produce in many Americans a general understanding of freedom as being able to do whatever one wants, but often without consideration of the consequences for others.

- Democratic societies also tend to strike the faith–reason tension on the side of reason and rationality. This is because of the centrality of science in modern democracies, which are sometimes referred to as the "rational regimes." But reason and rationality can be used in excessively narrow, bureaucratic, and instrumental ways, and when they take this form, they tend to undermine trust and the other social values that people need if they are to work together for the purpose of solving common problems.

- Our culture of freedom and radical individualism finds expression through television, the Internet, and the entertainment industry, and these influence young children's conceptions of freedom as well as their ideas of what other people are like. Children carry their conceptions into their classrooms and schools. Teachers respond by checking any disposition to indiscriminate self-expression and freedom, in part simply because they have to manage to teach 20 or more children at the same time in a single room. Teachers also, however, model the social virtues of trust, fairness, and the like, counteracting negative beliefs about human nature that children may have acquired from their culture; beliefs, for example, that people are only self-interested, always out for themselves, basically dishonest, and will take advantage of others when they can.

- The tensions in a democratic society's values are reflected in its teachers' values, often subtly but sometimes not. The purpose of the following chapters is to provide some empirical evidence of the effect that a democratic society has on its teachers, and to speculate about the effects they have on it, using America as a case in point.

NOTES

1. See S. H. Schwartz and W. Bilsky, "Toward a Universal Psychological Structure of Human Values," *Journal of Personality and Social Psychology* 53 (1987): 550–62.

2. Some philosophers have referred to these combinations as "cognitive-emotions." See Israel Scheffler, *In Praise of Cognitive Emotions and Other Essays* (New York: Routledge, 1991).

3. Howard Gardner, *Multiple Intelligences: New Horizons* (New York: Basic Books, 2006).

4. See "World Values Survey," World Values Survey Association, www.worldvaluessurvey.org/.

5. See Francis Fukuyama, *Trust* (New York: Free Press, 1995).

6. See Max Weber, *The Protestant Ethic and the Spirit of Capitalism* (New York: Dover, 2003), and Allan Bloom, *The Closing of the American Mind* (New York: Random House, 1987). See also Robert O. Slater, "Allan Bloom," in John Shook, ed., *The Dictionary of Modern American Philosophers* (Bristol, UK: Thoemmes Press, 2005), pp. 260–264.

Part II

TEACHERS' VALUES

Chapter Three

Family and Children's Values

FAMILY VALUES

The term "family values" has been central in the U.S. culture wars. Different groups often use the term to refer to different things, and when they do refer to the same issues they typically disagree about what policy should be with regard to them.[1]

Conservatives usually employ the phrase to promote censorship of sexual conduct on television and in the movies, laws against abortion and birth control, sexual abstinence outside of marriage, laws against same-sex marriage, and school prayer. When progressives use the term they usually do so in favor of family planning, contraception, abortion, sex education, maternity leave, child care, and, more recently, the normalization of same-sex relationships and marriage. Even when different groups use the term "family values" to refer to the same things, they often disagree over what the policies should be in relation to them.

In this chapter we will compare the positions of American elementary- and secondary-school teachers and Americans in general on marriage, divorce, premarital and extramarital sex, birth control, abortion, homosexuality, and pornography. We will also consider how important teachers think it is for children to learn to be independent and think for themselves, to work hard, to help others, to obey, and to be popular.

Marriage, Divorce and Separation

The institution of marriage, as everyone knows, has been on the decline in the United States but it has been less so for teachers than for other

33

Americans. In 1970s, for example, about 68 percent of adult Americans said they were married. By the 2012, the figure had fallen to around 46 percent. In just four decades, the number of Americans reporting themselves as being married dropped by more than 30 percent. Moreover, over the same four-decade period, the proportion of Americans who said they had never married almost doubled, going from about 14 percent in 1970s to about 27 percent in 2012.[2]

The percentage of married teachers, on the other hand, only dropped from 66 to 55 percent over the same four decades in question, just a 16 percent decline as compared to the 30 percent drop for the population as a whole. What is more, while the percent of teachers who said they had "never married" increased, just as it did for the general population, it did not double but only grew by about one-third, going from 16 percent in the 1970s to 21 percent in the 2000s. So while the data do support the oft-heard proposition that marriage has declined in America, it also indicates that the decline has been less for teachers than for other Americans.

When it comes to marriage, teachers have been more conservative.

Just as they are more likely than other Americans to marry, teachers, as a group have been less likely to get divorced or separated. If, for example, we examine the data over the entire four-decade period, 1972–2012, we find that proportionately fewer teachers than nonteachers have been divorced or separated. In the 1970s, for example, 15 percent of nonteachers reported being divorced or separated while only 6 percent of teachers did so.[3] The figures for each group rose during the 1980s, 1990s, and by the 2000s, one-quarter of nonteachers said they were divorced or separated. Still, only 18 percent of teachers said this (figure 3.1)

Premarital Sex

While nonteachers and teachers alike once felt that premarital sex was "always wrong," over the last forty years, nonteachers' views on the issue have grown more liberal while those of teachers have remained more conservative. In the 1970s, for example, about half of the teachers and nonteachers said that premarital sex was "always wrong." By the 2000s, however, only about one-third of nonteachers felt this way, while about 42 percent of teachers said this. Teachers, as a group, tend to be more conservative than other Americans about premarital sex.[4]

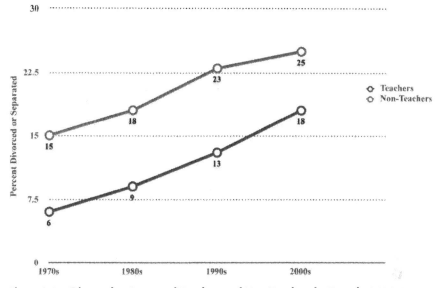

Figure 3.1.   Divorced or Separated Teachers and Non-Teachers by Decade (1972–2012).
Source: National Opinion Research Center, GSS, via the University of California at Berkeley, http://sda.
berkeley.edu/cgi-bin/hsda?harcsda+gss12.

Extramarital Sex

If one Googles the terms "adultery" or "extramarital sex," it is easy to find websites where it is claimed that 50 percent or more of Americans have been unfaithful to their spouses. The General Social Survey (GSS) data, however, tell a different story, one where the figures are much lower.

During the 1990s and 2000s, Americans were asked the question, "Have you ever had sex with someone other than your husband or wife while you were married?"

Combining the data for the 2000s, we find that 14 percent of Americans who were married or had been said that they had had an extramarital affair during their marriage. By contrast, however, only 8 percent of teachers said this. As a group, teachers report being less likely than nonteachers to stray from their marriages.[5]

Sex Education

The battle over whether the public discussion of sex should be restricted or open has been going on in America since the nineteenth century.

Moreover, the question of whether talk about sex should be allowed in the public schools in particular, and what form sex-talk in the classroom should take, has been controversial since the beginning of the twentieth.[6]

Sex education is controversial, of course, because it is not just about knowledge—facts about sexuality, sex, and intimate relationships—it is also about values, that is, judgments about which particular beliefs about sex and which sexual behaviors are deemed to be right and appropriate.

Much less controversial, however, has been public opinion about sex education generally. At least since the 1970s, 80 percent or more of Americans have been in favor of sex education in the public schools. However, beyond the general consensus that there should be some kind of sex education in the schools, there is sharp disagreement. The Left wants a more detailed or "comprehensive" approach. They want to recognize not only the role of abstinence but also call for the dissemination of more information about contraception. They also want condoms to be more available and distributed in schools.

For the conservatives, the devil really is in the comprehensive, "details" approach proposed by the Left. This is especially the case for the "just-say-no" Christian Right whose members advocate a general abstinence.

But where do teachers stand on the issue? Teachers tend to favor sex education. But they do so mainly because they are middle-class women with above-average educations. Their support of sex education really has nothing to do with their being teachers as such. However, when we control for gender, age, educational level, race, church attendance, income, and region of the country in which they live, we find that teachers, as teachers, tend to oppose sex education.[7]

Pornography

It is probably not too far off to say that pornography came of age in the United States in 1953 with the publication of the first issue of *Playboy* magazine. With its combination of photographs of nude women—often done by notable photographers—and articles by top literary writers, *Playboy* presented to a mass audience pornography with a patina of erotica, presumably in an effort to give it some artistic justification.

Playboy was soon followed in 1965 by more sexually explicit publications such as Bob Guccione's *Penthouse*, originally published in the

United Kingdom but later sold in the United States. Still later, in 1974, came Larry Flynt's *Hustler*, still more explicit and with no pretensions of being erotica or the least bit artistic. Since the 1970s, all of these and many other publications have become increasingly "hardcore" and have, with the advent of the Internet, morphed into pornographic sites that make the original *Playboy* appear almost naive.[8]

Perhaps some of the strongest opposition to the growth, development, and use of pornography in the United States has come from conservative Christian organizations, such as the American Family Association, from feminists, and from the U.S. government itself, the latter by way of various commissions and reports.[9]

The Belief that Pornography Breaks Down Morals

On the issue of pornography, teachers are more conservative than the general population. One of the most controversial issues pertaining to pornography is whether it leads to the breakdown of morals. From the 1970s to the 1990s, a growing proportion of both teachers and nonteachers said that it did. In the 1970s, 56 percent of teachers and 58 percent of Americans in general felt that pornography led to the breakdown of morals.

During the 1980s, both of these figures increased markedly. The percent of teachers believing this jumped to 75 percent while for other Americans it increased to 64 percent. During the 1990s, the percentage of teachers holding this view dropped a few points while for other Americans the proportion remained the same. So, as of the 1990s, three-fourths of American teachers and two-thirds of nonteachers believed that pornography led to the breakdown of morals. Teachers have been more conservative on the issue.

Should Pornography Be Outlawed?

There is a strong correlation between the belief that pornography leads to the breakdown of morals and the view that it should be made illegal to all, not only to those under 18 years of age. In the 1990s, for example, Americans who believed that pornography led to the breakdown of morals were four times as likely as those who did not believe this (54 vs. 13 percent) to say that pornography should be outlawed for everyone, not just those under 18.

Given the strong positive correlation between the belief in the harmful effects of pornography on morals, and also given that teachers tend to subscribe to this belief more than the general population, it is reasonable to suppose that a greater proportion of teachers than nonteachers would also think that pornography should be made illegal for everyone, young and old alike. This, indeed, is the case. Using the 2000–2010 data, we see that where only 36 percent of nonteachers believed that pornography should be made illegal to everyone, 46 percent of teachers believe it should be.

Not only, however, are teachers more conservative on the pornography issue, their views on the matter have been unchanged over the past four decades whereas the general population has grown more permissive. In the 1970s, for example, 42 percent of Americans said that pornography should be made illegal to all. By the 2000s, however, only 36 percent said this, a decline of 14 percent.

On the other hand, 47 percent of teachers during the 1970s said that pornography should be illegal across the board and nearly the same percentage said this in the 2000s. Unlike nonteachers, teachers, as a group, have not, over time, become more permissive of pornography. They have remained more conservative on the issue.

Abortion

In 2012, 44 percent of Americans said that a woman should be allowed to have an abortion for any reason; the majority of Americans are opposed to abortion on demand. But Americans' views on abortion greatly depend on their level of education.

The more educated Americans are, the more they tend to believe that a woman should be allowed to obtain an abortion for any reason. In 2012, for example, 73 percent of Americans with a graduate degree would allow a woman to have an abortion for any reason, while only 36 percent of those with a high-school education or less would. The most highly educated Americans were almost 40 percentage points more likely to allow abortion on demand than the least-educated Americans.

Given the education–abortion link, then, we could reasonably expect teachers to be inclined to allow abortion on demand, for they tend to have high levels of education.

But this is not the case. Not only do the majority of teachers oppose abortion on demand, but they are also more likely to oppose it than other highly educated Americans. As table A3.4 in the Appendix suggests, teachers, Americans who attend church one or more times per week, and Southerners tend to oppose abortion on demand while women and highly educated Americans are more inclined to allow it than are men and Americans with less education.

Homosexuality

Throughout the 1970s and 1980s, American teachers were more conservative than other adult Americans on the question of whether homosexuality is wrong. But by the 1990s, they were more in step with public opinion on the matter. But while teachers had grown as liberal as nonteachers on the homosexuality issue, they remained more conservative than other college-educated Americans. They were as liberal as the general population but not as liberal as other Americans who had been schooled as much as they had been. In other words, here we find a duality in the teachers' value system: they are at once progressive and conservative, progressive in relation to the general adult population with whom they came into contact with and taught, but conservative as compared to Americans equally well-educated (figure 3.2).

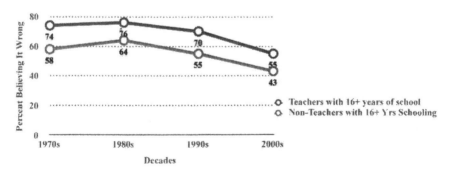

Figure 3.2. Belief that Homosexuality is "always wrong" by Teachers and Non-Teachers by Decade (1972–2012).
Source: National Opinion Research Center, GSS, via the University of California at Berkeley, http://sda. berkeley.edu/cgi-bin/hsda?harcsda+gss12.

CHILDREN'S VALUES

Hard Work?

America was built, it is often said, on a strong work ethic. Hard work was valued highly. But do Americans in general and teachers in particular believe that hard work is the most important value for children to learn? The short answer is that, no, they do not.

"Work is difficult," Seymour Martin Lipset reminds us, "and the question is not why people are lazy or why they goof off but why, in absence of compulsion, they work hard."[10] An important reason why early Americans worked hard, the sociologist Max Weber famously explained in his *The Protestant Work Ethic and the Spirit of Capitalism*, had to do with their religious beliefs.[11] The old Protestant religion, he said, treated work as not just a job but as a "calling," and success in one's work was believed to be a sign that one had been predestined for salvation. Thus was the work ethic in America rooted in the promise of salvation.

Complaints about the decline of the American work ethic are common but usually exaggerated. The Protestant work ethic has declined from its original intensity but it remains strong nonetheless. As Lipset puts it, "While the old-time Protestant ethic may have grown weaker, it is still much stronger in the United States than in other Christian nations, the United States being among the most religious, most observant, most deeply believing country in Christendom."[12]

Given the history of the value of work in America, we would expect teachers and nonteachers alike to believe that it is an important value for children to acquire. Moreover, given the unique role that teachers play in transmitting the nation's core values from one generation to the next, we might reasonably expect a greater percentage of teachers than nonteachers to think it an important quality for children to have.

Americans on Most Important Children's Qualities

Hard work is among five values for which the GSS contains data. These are: "to work hard," "to think for oneself," "to help others," "to obey," and "to be popular."

Figure 3.3 shows what percentage of Americans consider each of these five values to be "most important." From the figure we can see that the largest proportion of Americans (47 percent) said that, of the five qualities,

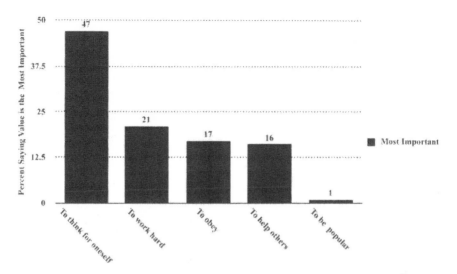

Figure 3.3. Five Values that Americans Believe Are Most Important for Children to Have (2000–2012).
Source: National Opinion Research Center, GSS, via the University of California at Berkeley, http://sda. berkeley.edu/cgi-bin/hsda?harcsda+gss12.

"to think for oneself" was the most important. This was more than twice as many who chose "to work hard" (21 percent). These two values are then followed in importance by "to obey" and "to help others" (17 and 16 percent). The value judged to be least important of the five was "to be popular."

Teachers, as it turns out, do not differ significantly from the rest of Americans on the value of hard work. They do, however, tend to value "to think for oneself" more highly than other Americans, as 60 percent of them say it is most important.

How Other Cultures Value Children's Qualities

Now, how do Americans' assessment of the value of these qualities stack up to the assessments of citizens from other nations? Hard work and the other four qualities or their near-equivalents are also part of the World Values Survey (WVS).[13] In the WVS, adults from 57 countries were asked which of these as well as other qualities they deemed "especially important" for children to learn. What proportion of the populations of other countries felt these qualities to be especially important and where does the United States stand in the global rankings?

Table 3.1 ranks all 57 countries by the percentage of the population in each which said that a particular quality was especially important. From

Table 3.1. Rankings of 57 Countries on Percentage of Their Populations Designating Each of Five Values as "Especially Important"

	Hard Work	Independence	Obedience	Religious Faith	Unselfishness
1	China (90)	Norway (91.2)	Ghana (81.7)	Indonesia (91.3)	Uruguay (61.4)
2	Georgia (90)	Slovenia (84.2)	Rwanda (78.8)	Iraq (90.6)	Peru (60.1)
3	Vietnam (89)	Indonesia (82.6)	Iraq (73.9)	Egypt (89.9)	Jordan (56)
4	Russian Federation (88.9)	Japan (80.7)	Trinidad & Tobago (72.3)	Jordan (84)	France (55.1)
5	Bulgaria (88.3)	Taiwan (80.4)	Burkina Faso (70.5)	Ghana (72.6)	Great Britain (55)
6	Romania (84.9)	Ethiopia (79.2)	Zambia (68)	Iran (72.1)	Australia (53.9)
7	Rwanda (83.1)	Malaysia (78.7)	Egypt (67.7)	Trinidad & Tobago (68.9)	Colombia (53.4)
8	India (81.7)	Germany (78)	Jordan (64.9)	Morocco (68.2)	Egypt (51.3)
9	Zambia (81.4)	Switzerland (77.9)	Colombia (59.2)	Burkina Faso (58.1)	Japan (50.7)
10	Burkina Faso (80.4)	Sweden (77.4)	Mexico (58.7)	Georgia (67.8)	Bulgaria (50.4)
11	Moldova (79.4)	China (75.4)	Brazil (56.8)	Romania (64)	Rwanda (50.1)
12	Turkey (79.2)	Finland (69.5)	India (56.2)	Mali (61.8)	Mexico (47.9)
13	Ghana (79.1)	India (67.2)	Thailand (54.7)	Zambia (61.1)	Canada (47.1)
14	Ukraine 78.7	Netherlands (67.2)	Mali (54.2)	Malaysia (59.6)	Italy (44.2)
15	Mali (75.3)	South Korea (66.3)	Peru (54.2)	Guatemala (58.7)	Cyprus (43.6)
16	South Korea (73.1)	Serbia (64.3)	Indonesia (53.7)	South Africa (56.2)	Guatemala (41.7)
17	South Africa (70.7)	Australia (64)	Chile (51.9)	Brazil (55.9)	Brazil (40.3)
18	Iran (69.5)	Iran (63.7)	Ukraine (51.2)	United States (50.8)	New Zealand (40)
19	Serbia (67.9)	Vietnam (59.5)	Morocco (50.9)	Colombia (47.7)	Burkina Faso (39.4)
20	Iraq (63.9)	Great Britain (58.9)	Cyprus (49.9)	Poland (46.7)	Slovenia (38.4)
21	Trinidad & Tobago (63.9)	Italy (58.9)	Poland (48.8)	Peru (45.3)	Zambia (37.9)
22	Spain (63.1)	South Africa (58.8)	South Africa (46.8)	Cyprus (42.3)	United States (37.8)
23	France (62.2)	Canada (58.1)	Guatemala (46.5)	Turkey (42.3)	Morocco (36.6)
24	United States (62)	New Zealand (55.3)	Great Britain (46.2)	Moldova (41.6)	Ethiopia (36.2)
25	Brazil (61.3)	Zambia (54.9)	Turkey (46)	India (41.5)	Mali (35.1)
26	Andorra (60.1)	Trinidad & Tobago (54.8)	Argentina (44.8)	Ethiopia (41.3)	Sweden (34.9)
27	Indonesia (59.9)	Morocco (54.8)	Serbia (44.3)	Chile (39.7)	China (34.9)
28	Argentina (58)	United States (54.1)	France (41.2)	Mexico (39.1)	India (34.4)

#					
29	Egypt (57.1)	Georgia (54.1)	Netherlands (40.2)	Rwanda (37.6)	Spain (33.8)
30	Taiwan (54.8)	Uruguay (49.4)	Italy (39.6)	Italy (34.6)	Vietnam (33.4)
31	Peru (54.6)	Thailand (49)	Australia (39)	Canada (30.4)	Ghana (33.1)
32	Ethiopia (54.5)	Andorra (48.5)	Ethiopia (38.9)	Thailand (30)	Serbia (32.9)
33	Canada (54.2)	Cyprus (46.9)	Uruguay (38.7)	Argentina (25.7)	Indonesia (32.8)
34	Morocco (51)	Bulgaria (46.8)	Andorra (38.4)	Serbia (25.2)	Iran (32.8)
35	Malaysia (49.1)	Argentina (44.2)	Russian Federation (38)	South Korea (21.7)	Moldova (32.3)
36	Australia (48.9)	Moldova (44)	Spain (37.2)	Australia (21.1)	Chile (31.8)
37	Cyprus (45.7)	Mali 43.8)	Finland (32.8)	Great Britain (18.8)	Thailand (31.6)
38	Great Britain (43.6)	Jordan (42.8)	Iran (32.7)	Bulgaria (18.5)	Turkey (31.4)
39	New Zealand (42.7)	Russian Federation (41.4)	Vietnam (32)	Uruguay (18.3)	South Africa (30.6)
40	Jordan (42.6)	Mexico (41.1)	Slovenia (31.7)	Slovenia (16.5)	Finland (30.2)
41	Italy (39.6)	Poland (41.1)	Canada (29.9)	Ukraine (16)	Taiwan (30.2)
42	Slovenia (34.1)	Chile (40.3)	Norway (29.1)	New Zealand (15.1)	Malaysia (30.1)
43	Japan (32.7)	Turkey (39.4)	United States (28.4)	Switzerland (12.6)	Netherlands (25.2)
44	Netherlands (29.6)	Ghana (37.2)	Malaysia (25.9)	Finland (12)	Trinidad & Tobago (23.7)
45	Guatemala (28.8)	France (37.2)	New Zealand (25.4)	Spain (11.3)	Romania (23.6)
46	Chile (27.2)	Colombia (33.5)	Bulgaria (25)	Russian Federation (11)	Norway (20.1)
47	Germany (26.1)	Spain (31.7)	Georgia (22)	Netherlands (9.8)	Russian Federation (19.6)
48	Mexico (24.5)	Burkina Faso (31.2)	Switzerland (18.5)	Germany (9.4)	Andorra (18.7)
49	Thailand (23.3)	Romania (29.7)	Romania (17.8)	Taiwan (8.9)	Poland (18.1)
50	Uruguay (22.4)	Iraq (29.1)	Moldova (16.8)	France (8.7)	Georgia (17.1)
51	Poland (21.3)	Ukraine (28.8)	Taiwan (16.5)	Norway (8.7)	Switzerland (14.3)
52	Switzerland (20.3)	Brazil (28.6)	China (16.1)	Andorra (6.9)	Ukraine (13.5)
53	Colombia (19)	Guatemala (27.9)	Germany (15.9)	Sweden (6.1)	South Korea (11.7)
54	Hong Kong (18.9)	Peru (27.6)	Sweden (15.6)	Vietnam (6.1)	Iraq (9.5)
55	Finland (14.7)	Egypt (26.7)	South Korea (13.6)	Japan (5.6)	Argentina (8.7)
56	Norway (12.9)	Rwanda (25.6)	Japan (5.2)	China (2.4)	Germany (6.8)
57	Sweden (10.6)	Hong Kong (24.2)	Hong Kong (2.3)	Hong Kong (1.2)	Hong Kong (1.8)

Source: World Values Survey Association

the table we can see that—proportionately more than any other peoples—the Chinese (90.2 percent), said that "hard work" was especially important for children to learn. On this quality, the United States, with 62 percent, ranked 24th out of the 57 countries surveyed.

The WVS does not have a question that specifically asks whether "to think for oneself" should be an important quality for children to acquire—the quality Americans value most—but it does include "independence" on its list, and the two would seem to be closely related if not identical in meaning. Norway ranked first on this one, with 91.2 percent of its people feeling that this was an especially important quality while the United States ranked 28th with 54.1 percent.

Among the five qualities, The United States' highest ranking was on "Religious Faith." Among the Christian countries, the United States ranks third behind Romania and Brazil in having a population that believes religious faith is especially important for children to learn. However, the most religious countries, on this score, are Indonesia, followed closely by Iraq and Egypt.

Among the five qualities we have been considering as important for children to learn, "obedience" was the quality garnering the least endorsement by the adults in the 57 countries in the study. On this quality, the United States ranked 43rd with 28 percent of adults approving it. Ghana, on the other hand, ranked first and Hong Kong and Japan came in at the lowest end of the range.

POINTS TO REMEMBER

- For most if not all of the last four decades, American teachers have been more likely to be married, and less likely to be divorced.
- Teachers tend to frown on premarital sex and, as a group, say they have been less likely to stray from their marriage commitments.
- Teachers tend to favor sex education though not because of anything having to do with their being teachers but more so because of their being middle-class, highly educated women.
- Teachers are opposed to pornography and believe it leads to the breakdown of morals, not only of those under the age of 18, but everyone's.
- Teachers, as a group, tend to be opposed to abortion on demand.

- When it comes to family values, elementary and secondary teachers are often more liberal than the general adult population but more conservative than comparably educated nonteachers. They are, in relation to the value system as a whole, a liberal force but in relation to college-educated nonteachers, their impact is conservative.

- This duality of teachers' values is noteworthy because almost all members of modern societies come into contact with teachers, whose occupation has as one of its missions the transmission of values, a mission that can be claimed by no other occupation with such a large and captive audience. Teachers push one group toward change while they simultaneously hold the other to tradition. They function as a society's values governors.

NOTES

1. "Are 'Family Values' Outdated?" *New York Times*, April 24, 2012, www. nytimes.com/roomfordebate/2012/04/24/are-family-values-outdated/the-myth-of-the-traditional-family.

2. Unless otherwise noted, all of the percentage differences reported in this book are statistically significant at the .05 level or less. The GSS variables used in the calculations are "teachers," "decades," and "marital." "Teachers" is a recoded variable using the three occupational census variables: "occ," "occ80," and "occ10." Only kindergarten, elementary-, and secondary-school teachers are included. "Decades" is recoded using the variable "year."

3. The GSS variables used here are "teachers," "marital," "divorce," and "decades2" where the category "2000s" in "decades2" includes data from 2012.

4. The percentage differences reported here and elsewhere throughout the chapter were obtained with cross-tabulation in which, again, the results were statistically significant. These results were then put into a logistic regression model wherein gender, age, education, race, class, and region of residence were included as control variables. See table A3.1 in the Appendix for this analysis.

5. For the Logistic regression, see table A3.2 in the Appendix.

6. Janice M. Irvine, *Talk about Sex: The Battles over Sex Education in the United States* (Berkeley: University of California Press, 2002), 4.

7. See table A3.3 for the logistic regression.

8. See Frederick S. Lane, *Obscene Profits: The Entrepreneurs of Pornography in the Cyber Age* (New York: Routledge, 2001).

9. Dick Thornburgh and Herbert Lin, "Youth, Pornography and the Internet" (Washington, DC: National Research Council, 2002).

10. Seymour Martin Lipset, "The Work Ethic, Then and Now," *Journal of Labor Research* 13 (1992): 45.

11. Max Weber, *The Protestant Work Ethic and the Spirit of Capitalism* (New York: Dover, 2003).

12. Lipset, "The Work Ethic," 52.

13. "World Values Survey," World Values Survey Association, www.world-valuessurvey.org/.

Chapter Four

Religion

One of the primary tensions at work in modern democratic societies is that between traditional values and secularism. This tension, most sharply defined, is between religion and reason or religion and science, religion being the most traditional value of all, and science being the highest form of reason. Modern democracies are the "regimes of reason," and in these societies the legitimacy of rationality, law, administration, and bureaucracy tends to be primary, that of religion secondary.[1] Nonetheless, religion and belief in God are still held to be important by many citizens of modern democratic states. This seems to be especially the case than in the United States.

In the World Values Survey, 47 percent of the U.S. population said that God was very important in their lives, a greater percentage by far than the populations of such other developed countries as Great Britain (21 percent), Canada (32), France (13), Italy (34), Australia (19), Spain (15), or Germany (11).[2] God and religion obviously play an important role in the lives of almost half of Americans. Accordingly, we would expect religion to play an important role in the lives of American teachers.

Religion and education have always had a close relationship in the United States. The first university in the United States, Harvard College, was established in 1636 to train ministers. Many of the country's first teachers were ministers and parsons. Even when women came to dominate the teaching field, religious values were still dominant. Given the important role of religion in the United States and the historic relationship between religion and education in the United States, we should not be surprised if we find that elementary- and secondary-school teachers place a high priority on religion.

RELIGIOUS PREFERENCE

We can begin by simply noting religious preference. As of the 2012 General Social Survey (GSS), 44 percent of Americans reported themselves as being Protestant, 24 percent as Catholic, and 1 percent as Jewish. Roughly 20 percent said that they have no religious preference at all. The remaining 11 percent include Buddhist, Hindus, Moslems, Native Americans, and others who identify themselves as simply Christian or Orthodox-Christian.

With one exception, the proportion of teachers in each of these religious groups does not seem to differ significantly from that of the general population. For example, 44 percent of teachers said they were Protestants, a figure equal to that of nonteachers. The proportion of teachers who were Catholic was also about the same as that of the proportion of nonteachers who reported being a Catholic. The one exception was that 4 percent of teachers reported being Jewish, a greater percentage than in the general population.

CHURCH ATTENDANCE

We can get a better idea of how religious teachers are by looking at their church going habits. Do teachers attend church more or less often than other Americans? If we look at the data from 2000–2012, we find that 36 percent of teachers said they went to church one or more times per week whereas only 26 percent of nonteachers reported going this often. Moreover, if we control for education and compare teachers with only nonteachers with bachelor's degrees or higher, we still find that a greater percentage of teachers attend church more frequently (36 vs. 28 percent). By this measure, teachers seem to be more religious than other Americans.

Teachers frequent church-going has varied over the last 40 years. The proportion of them who attended church frequently was highest in the 1980s, during the Reagan administration. During this decade, 46 percent of teachers said they attended church one or more times per week as compared to 30 percent of highly educated nonteachers.

Why do teachers attend church more than other Americans? Gender seems to be a factor. Most teachers are women and women tend to go to church more often than men. In the 2010–2012 data, for example, 23 percent of men but 29 percent of women said they attended church one or more times per week. Perhaps teachers are more religious simply because most teachers are women and women are more religious than men, or at least they attend church services more frequently.

When we control for gender, however, we find that, in the 2006–2012 data, not only women teachers tend to go to church more often than women nonteachers (34 vs. 29 percent), but also men teachers tend to attend church more often than male nonteachers (35 vs. 22 percent). Gender does not appear to be the key factor that explains teachers' religiousness. Even among teachers and nonteachers of the same gender, teachers tend to go to church more. They are more religious (see table A4.1 in Appendix).

PRAYER

Another indicator that teachers tend to be more religious is that, as a group, they tend to pray more often than other Americans. Restricting our analysis to the 2010 and 2012 GSS surveys, we find that 34 percent of teachers say they pray "several times a day," while only about 28 percent of nonteachers with only high-school education or less, and about 22 percent of the college-educated nonteachers, say they do this. Moreover, with more advanced methods of analysis we can see that there is a very strong and significant relationship between being a teacher and praying frequently (see table A4.2 in the Appendix). Accordingly, we can be confident in saying teachers tend to pray more than other Americans and are therefore more religious.

HOW FUNDAMENTALIST ARE AMERICAN TEACHERS?

Obviously, Christian fundamentalists value religion. Two basic beliefs or doctrines characterize Christian fundamentalism in America. One is the inerrancy of Scripture which "has been interpreted variously, but generally it holds that the written text of the Bible was inspired by God, that the Bible is thus a record of the actual, words of God, and that it therefore can be trusted to be infallible in all its details."

The second is the doctrine of dispensational premillennialism which divides history into distinct periods (dispensations) and "asserts that history as we know it will end with Jesus' literal return to earth, after which he will establish a godly kingdom that will last for a thousand years."[3] How fundamentalist are Americans in general and teachers in particular?

If we control for education and compare teachers with comparably educated Americans, we find that for each of the last four decades, 1972–2012, teachers have tended to be more fundamentalist than highly educated nonteachers (figure 4.1).

REGIONALISM

As might be expected, religious fundamentalism tends to be more pronounced in the South, and here, too, we find the largest concentration of fundamentalist teachers. A little over one-third of Southern teachers say they are fundamentalist as compared to 11 percent in the Northeast, 20 percent in the Midwest, and 21 percent in the West.

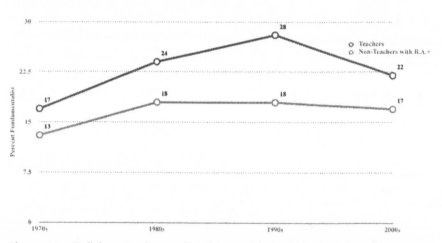

Figure 4.1. Religious Fundamentalism by Teachers and Non-Teachers by Decades (1972–2012).
Source: National Opinion Research Center, GSS, via the University of California at Berkeley, http://sda.berkeley.edu/cgi-bin/hsda?harcsda+gss12.

PRAYER IN PUBLIC SCHOOLS

Where do school teachers stand on the school prayer issue? More specifically, do they approve or disapprove of the U.S. Supreme Court's ruling that prohibits prayer in public schools? Given the priority that teachers tend to give to religion, we might reasonably expect to find them more disapproving of the ruling than other Americans.

At the same time, however, teachers have a relatively high level of education, and the more education Americans have the more they tend to approve of the Supreme Court's ban on school prayer. Figure 4.2 shows that, on this issue, too, teachers tend to straddle the middle of the value system, being more liberal than Americans with less education than they have but more conservative than comparably educated Americans.

POINTS TO REMEMBER

- As a group, teachers appear to be more religious than other Americans. A greater percentage of teachers than nonteachers attend church one or more times per week, and a greater percentage, as well, pray "several times a day."

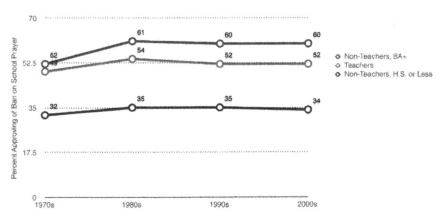

Figure 4.2. Approve of Supreme Court's Ban on School Prayer by Teachers and Non-Teachers (1972–2012).
Source: National Opinion Research Center, GSS, via the University of California at Berkeley, http://sda.berkeley.edu/cgi-bin/hsda?harcsda+gss12.

- When it comes to religious fundamentalism, teachers in this case, too, tend to straddle the middle. They are less fundamentalist, percentage wise, than the least-educated Americans but they are more so than the best-educated Americans. Moreover, the highest concentration of fundamentalist teachers is in the South. About one-third of the teachers living there say they are fundamentalists.
- Finally, when it comes to the issue of school prayer, teachers again straddle the middle. They are more likely to approve of the Supreme Court's ban on school prayer than Americans having less education but they are less likely to do so than nonteachers who are college-educated.

NOTES

1. The term "rational regime" is generally attributed to Leo Strauss, whose student, Allan Bloom, used it to some effect in his *Closing of the American Mind* (New York: Random House, 1987), 196ff.

2. World Values Survey Association, World Values Survey, 2006, www .wvsevsdb.com/wvs/WVSAnalizeQuestion.jsp.

3. Robert Wuthnow, "The World of Fundamentalism, 1992, www.religion online.org/showarticle.asp?title=230.

Chapter Five

The Social Values

Community grows out of the human capacity and need for communication and cooperation. It has long been felt to be basic to human development and growth. Civil society, a modern variant, is believed to be fundamental to the development and maintenance of democracy.

However, for people to have things in common, to create community, they must, as John Dewey says, communicate.[1] But their willingness and capacity to do so depends on the extent to which they value certain "social virtues," as they are sometimes called.[2] These are such things as the belief that people can be trusted, that they are basically helpful, and that they are fair.

The more that people believe in or value these things, the more likely they will actualize them by communicating. Furthermore, as a result of this interaction and the understanding that flows from it, the greater the possibility that a community will be formed and sustained. To what degree, then, do Americans in general and teachers in particular value trust, helpfulness, and fairness?

TRUST

The year 1995 saw the publications of two important works on trust, Robert Putnam's "Bowling Alone" and Francis Fukyama's *Trust*.[3] Putnam's work was important in part because in it he claimed that trust levels in America were on the decline, a fact that did not bode well for "social capital," a term used to refer to Americans' willingness and capacity to

come together—especially outside of government-sponsored agencies—
to solve common problems.[4]

Social capital is itself important, Putnam pointed out, because it influences civil society—the matrix of informal relationships and systems of
communication—that enable formal economic and political action to be
carried on. Some of the data that Putnam used to make his point about
declines in trust he took from the General Social Survey (GSS), one of
the sources we are using in this book, though he did not have, in the early
1990s, as many years of data as we now have for analysis.

Fukuyama's book on trust was important because it developed more
fully the link between trust and economies and polities, particularly those
that happen to be democratic. He says that "one of the most important lessons we can learn from an examination of economic life is that a nation's
well-being, as well as its ability to compete, is conditioned by a single
pervasive cultural characteristic: the level of trust inherent in society."[5]

The link between trust and democracy seems especially important in
our time as the fortunes of democracy have lately been cast into doubt.
In recent years, political democracy—the competitive and open election
of public officials by a largely enfranchised population—has declined in
more countries than it has advanced.[6]

The decline of political democracy in the 2000s marks a sharp rever-
sal from the democratization trends of the 1990s when some democracy
scholars were so optimistic they were writing that "The world . . . is in
the grip of a democratic revolution. Throughout the developing world . . .
nations are on the march toward democracy." Fukuyama himself picked
up on a Hegelian theme and wrote that we had finally arrived at the "End
of History," meaning that in democracy history had reached a phase of
political development on which there could be no further progress.[7,8]

Not all scholars were as caught up in the early 1990s democratic eupho-
ria, however. Fareed Zakaria, for example, had observed that while many
of the newly democratic countries possessed the minimum criteria to be
considered democratic, they still fell considerably short of the democratic
ideal.[9]

Now, in the wake of movements in Venezuela, Ecuador, and Bolivia, as
well as elsewhere in the world, the mood has turned more pessimistic. As
Bruce Gilley has observed, "The hottest books on democratization these
days concern not democratic advance but authoritarian resurgence."[10]

The degree to which individuals trust one another, then, is not simply important for individual well-being but figures importantly into community and, ultimately, national well-being too. It would appear to be particularly important in education because schools provide our youth, as we have already noted, with some of their most intense and prolonged experiences, and among these experiences surely are included experience of the "social virtues," experiences they likely obtain from interacting with teachers whose levels of trust, as we shall see, are higher than those of most other Americans. Accordingly, teacher trust is no small thing.

Since Putnam and Fukuyama brought the issue of trust to the forefront of the American consciousness, a great deal of work has been done on the topic in education. The early work in this context often focused on the effects of teacher trust on students and parents.[11] In much of this research, trust has been viewed as one of the characteristics of schools that make a difference for the achievement of all students.[12] However, less work has been done on the effects of teacher trust on the formation in our children of the foundations of social capital.

U.S. TRUST LEVELS COMPARED TO OTHER COUNTRIES

One of Robert Putnam's main findings in his study of declining social capital in America was that U.S. trust levels had declined.[13] Recent GSS data mirror what Putnam found in 1995, and shows that trust levels have dropped over the last four decades, going from 46 percent in 1972 to 32 percent in 2012, a 30 percent decline (figure 5.1).

Only about one-third of Americans, then, say that other people can be trusted. But how do American trust levels compare with those of other countries? The World Values Survey (WVS) contains a question on trust, and provides responses from adults of 57 different countries, including the United States. These data, like the GSS, are conveniently available online 24/7 at www.worldvaluessurvey.org/.

From the WVS data we find that Norway has the highest trust levels. Almost three-fourths of the Norwegians think that people can be trusted, more than twice the percentage of Americans who feel this way.

Close behind Norway is Sweden, with 68 percent of its general population saying this, and 77.8 percent of its college-educated population. They

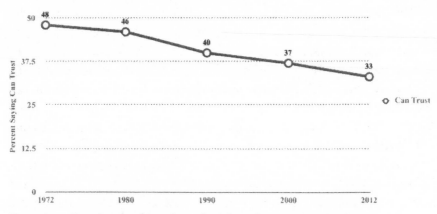

Figure 5.1.   Trust Levels of Americans for Selected Years (1972–2012).
Source: National Opinion Research Center, GSS, via the University of California at Berkeley, http://sda.
berkeley.edu/cgi-bin/hsda?harcsda+gss12.

are followed by Finland (58.9 percent), Switzerland (53.9), and China
(52.3), to round out the top five. About 70 percent of the most highly
educated Chinese, by the way, believe that people can be trusted. At the
other end of the scale, the country with the lowest levels of trust, by the
WVS measure, is Trinidad and Tobago (3.8 percent) and it is followed by
Turkey (4.9), Rwanda (4.9), Ghana (8.5), and Malaysia (8.8).

Trust levels for the United States as a whole are at 39.3 percent in the
WVS survey, a little higher than the 32 percent we find in the GSS, but
not dramatically so. The average for all of the countries included in the
WVS surveys is 26.1 percent. So, compared to these countries, the United
States appears to be above the average on trust. However, U.S. trust levels
are not as high as some other developed countries with which the United
States is often compared.

AMERICAN TEACHERS' TRUST LEVELS

Now, how do the trust levels of American teachers compare with those of
other Americans? In 2012, 52 percent of teachers said that people could
be trusted while only 33 percent of nonteachers said this. Teachers tend
to be more trusting than other Americans.

We know, however, that trust is highly correlated with education and, as it turns out, teachers tend to have high trust levels largely because they have more education than most Americans.

A Gallup survey done in 2009 found that education, income, race, and age affect levels of trust.[14] The more education Americans have, for example, the more likely they are to be trusting. In 2012, for instance, about one-quarter of Americans with a high-school education or less said that people could be trusted while, by contrast, 54 percent of Americans with a bachelor's degree or higher said this. The most highly educated Americans were more than twice as likely as their least educated counterparts to trust others. Education has a significant impact on Americans' willingness to trust.

Teachers tend to have university degrees, so given the strong link between education and trust we should not be surprised to find that teachers are more trusting than Americans with only a high-school education or less. In 2012, about 58 percent of American teachers said that people could be trusted but only 25 percent of nonteachers with a high-school education or less said this.

Teachers' trust levels appear to be largely a result of their education and they are no more or less trusting than other highly educated Americans. However, teachers encounter all of America's children, whereas other highly educated Americans do not. To understand the significance of this, we need to recall that, as of 2012, only 10 percent of parents who had a high-school education or less and also had children under the age of six said that people could be trusted.

Why so many Americans with this little education and young children have low trust levels is a question that need not distract us at this juncture. The point to be made with this fact is that not until they reach school will many of these children likely have their first intensive and sustained experience of adults who trust others.

TRUST LEVELS OF TEACHERS
VERSUS 18- TO 24-YEAR-OLDS

The relatively high trust levels of American teachers are also important in light of the low trust levels of American 18- to 24-year-olds, levels that have declined over the past 40 years. Teachers, as a group, have been more than twice as likely as our youth to believe that people are trustworthy. Combining the surveys from the years 2006 to 2012, for example, we find that over half of the teachers said they could trust people while only 17 percent of our 18- to 24-year-olds said this.[15] Again, as teachers value trust relatively highly, they stand to influence our youth to be more trusting, an effect that holds implications for the health of American civil society.

COOPERATION AND HELPFULNESS

Are People Helpful or Only Out for Themselves?

Community depends on people's willingness to communicate but it also depends on their capacity and desire to cooperate. As any experienced and effective leader knows, what from point of view of leadership may appear as a problem of coordination, from the perspective of the followers always appears as a question of cooperation. Unless people are willing to follow, to cooperate, there can be no effective leadership. Moreover, cooperation and a willingness to be helpful are closely aligned. If people are not willing to help, they will not cooperate.

Our disposition to be helpful depends in no small way on whether or not we believe that other people are disposed to be helpful. The more people believe that others are not helpful, the less inclined they themselves are to help. Accordingly, the degree to which people in a society are willing to be helpful depends on their perceptions of others. Additionally, just as teachers serve as role models of trust, so also they act as role models for helpfulness and cooperation. Accordingly, their beliefs about whether or not people are basically helpful are important.

From 1973 to 2010, Americans have been asked the following question: "Would you say that most of the time people try to be helpful, or that they are mostly just looking out for themselves?" Looking at the 2006 to 2012 survey results, we find that 72 percent of teachers said that people try to be helpful as compared to 43 percent of nonteachers with high-school educations or less and 63 percent of college-educated nonteachers. Teachers are more likely than nonteachers to see people as helpful (figure 5.2)

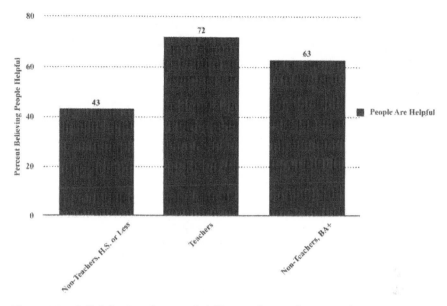

Figure 5.2. Belief that People are Helpful by Teachers and Non-Teachers (2006–2012)
Source: National Opinion Research Center, GSS, via the University of California at Berkeley, http://sda.
berkeley.edu/cgi-bin/hsda?harcsda+gss12.

Teachers are also more likely than 18- to 24-year-olds to see people as being helpful. Using the 2006–2012 survey results, only 34 percent of Americans between the ages of 18 and 24 saw people as helpful whereas, again, 70 percent of American teachers did.

FAIRNESS

Our perception of fairness in others, just as our perceptions of trust and helpfulness, influences our own disposition to be fair. The more we believe that other people are out to take advantage of us, the more difficult it is for us to be fair. Not only our common sense but also economic principles suggest this to be true.

We all try, the economists tell us, to make rational decisions, and reason tells us to protect ourselves from others who would take advantage of us. So, the more people believe others are out to take advantage, the less likely they are themselves to be fair. It is important, therefore, to know whether our teachers, who are primary role models for our children, believe that people are basically fair or out to take advantage.

From 1973 to 2012, Americans have been asked the following question: "Do you think most people would try to take advantage of you if they got a chance, or they would try to be fair?" Looking at just the survey results from 2006 to 2012 results, we find that 77 percent of teachers believe that people are fair whereas only 39 percent of 18- to 24-year-olds think so. Teachers are almost twice as likely as young people to believe that people are fair.

POINTS TO REMEMBER

- A healthy democracy needs social capital or people who are willing and able to come together voluntarily to solve common problems as in, for example, neighborhood associations. But social capital depends, in turn, on a number of key social values such as trust, helpfulness, fairness, and the like; people will not cooperate if they do not trust others or believe that others are out to take advantage of them.
- The social values such as trust and the like are not automatically acquired at birth but must be taught and learned. Children learn social values by observing and interacting with adults who themselves have high levels of trust, and who believe that being helpful, fair, and so on, are important.
- Teachers tend to be more trusting than other Americans and are more likely to see other people as being helpful and fair.
- Over the past four decades, the percentage of Americans who say that people can be trusted has declined in the United States, dropping from about 48 percent in 1973 to about 35 percent by 2010.
- For children from households where trust is low and people are viewed as not helpful nor fair, teachers provide adult models of trust, helpfulness, and fairness.
- The U.S. educational system is now caught up in a teacher-assessment movement where teaches are being judged on the "value they add" from one year to the next to their students' test scores.
- Test scores are important but so also are the effects that teachers have on children's willingness and capacity to learn to trust, to be helpful, and to be fair in their dealings with others.

- We need to understand better the effects that teachers have on children's acquisition of the social values.
- We need to understand better the effects of the "value-added" models of teacher assessment on teachers' levels of trust, cooperativeness, helpfulness, and belief in the fundamental fairness of things.

NOTES

1. John Dewey, *Democracy and Education* (New York: Free Press, 1917).

2. For a discussion of values, their actualization and their relation to virtues, and the role values play in individual and collective development, see David Norton's *Democracy and Moral Development* (Berkeley: University of California Press, 1992). On the social virtues, see Francis Fukuyama, *Trust* (New York: Free Press, 1995), 43.

3. See Robert Putnam, "Bowling Alone: America's Declining Social Capital," *Journal of Democracy* 6 (1995): 65–78 and Fukuyama, *Trust*.

4. The concept of social capital was early on developed by the University of Chicago professor James Coleman. See James Coleman, "Social Capital in the Creation of Human Capital," *The American Journal of Sociology* 94 (Supplement 1988): S95–S120. Coleman's work was later complimented by Robert Putnam's research. For Putnam's initial discussion, see Putnam, "Bowling Alone." For a recent application of the concept of social capital to teachers, see Cheri Hoff Minckler, "Teacher Social Capital: The Development of a Conceptual Model and Measurement Framework with Application to Educational Leadership and Teacher Efficacy," PhD diss., the University of Louisiana at Lafayette, 2011.

5. Fukuyama, *Trust*, 7.

6. Freedom House (2012), Freedom in the World: 2012, www.freedomhouse.org/report/freedom-world/freedom-world-2012.

7. Larry Diamond, "Three Paradoxes of Democracy," *Journal of Democracy* 1 (1990): 48.

8. Francis Fukuyama, *The End of History and the Last Man* (New York: Free Press, 1992).

9. Fareed Zakaria, "The Rise of Illiberal Democracy," *Foreign Affairs* 76 (1997): 22–43.

10. Bruce Gilley, "Democratic Triumph, Scholarly Pessimism," *Journal of Democracy* 21 (2010): 160–67.

11. See on this point Megan Tschannen-Moran, "Collaboration and the Need for Trust," *Journal of Educational Administration* 39 (2001): 308–31, and Roger D. Goddard, Megan Tschannen-Moran, and Wayne K. Hoy, "A Multilevel

Examination of the Distribution and Effects of Teacher Trust in Students and Parents in Urban Elementary Schools," *Elementary School Journal* 102 (2001): 3–17.

12. Wayne K. Hoy, "School Characteristics that Make a Difference for the Achievement of All Students: A 40-year Odyssey," *Journal of Educational Administration* 50 (2012): 76–97. See also Anthony Bryk and Barbara Schneider, *Trust in Schools: A Core Resource for Improvement* (New York: Russell Sage Foundation, 2002).

13. Putnam, "Bowling Alone."

14. Brent Pelham and Steve Crabtree, "In U.S., Trust Varies with Education, Income, Race and Age," Gallup Wellbeing, www.gallup.com/poll/124580/Trust-Varies-Income-Education-Race-Age.aspx.

15. The GSS variables here are "trust," recoded to eliminate the "depends" category; "year" = 2012; and "teachers3," a variable constructed from "teachers" and "age."

Chapter Six

Freedom

Our purpose in this chapter is to examine teachers' values as they pertain to freedom. Teachers continually strike a balance between continuity and change.[1] They play a dual role. They act, on the one hand, as agents of change while, on the other, they serve as keepers of tradition. They hold back or check the development of some values while encouraging and cultivating others. Freedom is one of the values they check.

We often speak of freedom in the abstract as if it were a single, monolithic thing, but the history of freedom, the human struggle for it, is in fact a history of a struggle not for freedom in general but for particular freedoms. The history of the rise of the democratic-liberal state, for example, is a history of how Parliament gradually won from the Crown one freedom after another, laying the foundation for the rise of the liberal state.[2]

Thus to ask whether or not someone values freedom or how much they value it is to ask, in the final analysis, how much they value particular freedoms. But, if this is so, then we need to decide which of the particular freedoms are the most important for our purposes.

WHICH FREEDOMS?

We have at least two important documents at our disposal to help us articulate what the most important freedoms are. These are the U.S. Bill of Rights, U.S. Constitution, and the United Nations Declaration of Human Rights.[3] Both of these documents are official declarations, emphatic statements or claims that certain specific freedoms are important enough that all peoples should aspire to them and all governments should respect and protect them.

From these two documents, we can draw up at least a working list of fundamental human rights or most basic freedoms. These include freedom of speech, opinion, and expression; freedom of belief, thought, conscience, and religion; freedom of movement within and across national borders; freedom to choose employment; freedom to marry whom we choose; freedom to participate in the cultural life of the community; freedom from fear; and freedom from want (see table 6.1).

This working list can serve as a useful guide for us in our effort to specify which freedoms are most valued or deemed most worthy not only because it closely aligns with what people understand freedom to be but also because it is derived from one document that is transnational, and therefore not specific to any particular culture, and from another that is specific to the American case.

But given this working list of freedoms, how can we tell how much a person values any of them? What can we use as indications of the importance a person attaches to these freedoms?

Our survey, the General Social Survey (GSS), contains some questions that enable us to present people with hypothetical situations involving issues and questions pertaining to these freedoms.

For example, we can ask respondents how they feel about free speech. We can ask whether or not they think that someone, say, a communist, atheist, homosexual, or racist should be free to do or say particular things in a particular situation. In this way we can more or less measure how much they value or think important another person's right to speak out on

Table 6.1. Basic Human Rights and Freedoms

—Freedom of speech, opinion, and expression
—Freedom of belief, thought, conscience, and religion
—Freedom of movement within and across national borders
—Freedom to choose employment
—Freedom to marry whom we choose
—Freedom to participate in the cultural life of the community
—Freedom from fear
—Freedom from want

Sources: United Nations, *Universal Declaration of Human Rights, 1948*, www.un.org/Overview/rights.html; U.S. National Archives and Records Administration, *The U.S. Constitution–Bill of Rights*, www.archives. gov/national-archives-experience/charters/bill_of_rights_transcript.html.

controversial issues, to teach, and to express their beliefs and thoughts by writing and publishing books.

We can also ask them about their attitudes toward authority and authority figures, their views of law enforcement and the like. In this way we can accumulate various indicators of how much teachers and Americans in general value "freedom." We turn now to this task.

FREEDOM OF SPEECH

Why is freedom of speech so important? Of all our capacities, speech is the one that perhaps most obviously distinguishes us from nonhuman beings. The children's classic *Dr. Doolittle* is but a charming reminder of this brute fact.[4] To the capacity for speech is tied many others, including language development and, through it, social relationships and culture. To deny someone the right to speak, therefore, is symbolically, at least, to deny them one of their most fundamentally human capacities; it is, in effect, to deny them their humanity.

On another level, freedom of speech is also necessary to guard against and oppose tyranny. The most important condition of democracy, even one of its defining characteristics, says John Dewey, is freedom of communication between and within groups, and speech is the first mode of communication.[5] Open communication allows the sharing of diverse experiences. Diversity of experience provides alternatives to what people know and the things with which they are familiar. Without alternatives, we see only the here-and-now. The capacity to question existing arrangements and ways of doing things is restrained or confined.

To deny free speech, then, is to undermine democracy by curtailing the communications structures and diversity of experiences and opinions that give rise to and sustain it.

An appreciation for and desire to honor and protect a person's right to speak freely makes a good measure of how much Americans in general and teachers in particular value freedom. This is especially the case the more repugnant and offensive the speech is.

Our capacity to value freedom rests mainly on our ability to reason and on our reasoning processes. When someone speaks out against what we hold most dear, our most natural response is to want to silence them. To refrain from doing so, and even to promote their right to say what grievously offends us, suggests that we have ourselves reflected and thought deeply about the issue of free speech, thereby enabling our reason and reasoning processes to outweigh our natural emotional response.

How much importance, then, do Americans in general and American teachers in particular attach to free speech? We can begin by examining data on how Americans and American teachers feel about the free speech rights of four controversial types: a communist, atheist, racist, and homosexual. From 1972 until as recently as 2012, Americans have been asked the following questions:

Now I should like to ask you some questions about a man who admits he is a Communist. (Atheist, Racist, Homosexual) Suppose this admitted Communist (Atheist, Racist, Homosexual) wanted to make a speech in your community. Should he be allowed to speak or not?

A. Suppose he is teaching in a college. Should he be fired, or not?

B. Suppose he wrote a book which is in your public library. Somebody in your community suggests that the book should be removed from the library. Would you favor removing it, or not?

Let us first consider the communist. Have teachers been more likely than nonteachers to say that they would allow an admitted communist to give a speech in their community? If we take data from all of the surveys (1972–2012) and organize them into decades, we find that from the 1970s to the 2000s, a greater percentage of teachers than nonteachers would allow a communist to speak.

In the 1970s, for example, 68 percent of teachers would allow him or her to speak while only 58 percent of nonteachers would. By the 2000s, Americans in general and teachers in particular had grown more liberal on the question. By then 77 percent of teachers would let the communist speak as compared to 68 percent of nonteachers. Nonetheless, while both groups had grown more liberal over the four-decade period, teachers were still more likely than nonteachers to support free speech.

This suggests that, where the value of freedom is concerned, and particularly in relation to the general population, teachers would seem to endorse change—movement toward more freedom, not less.

This is not, however, the whole story. As it turns out, education itself plays a role in how willing Americans are to support the free-speech rights of a communist (or others, for that matter).

The more education people have, the more likely they are to support free speech. In 2012, for example, only about 44 percent of Americans with less than a high-school education would allow a communist to speak but 87 percent of those who had a bachelor's degree would (figure 6.1). Moreover, the proportion of the most educated Americans who would is still higher. Among those with a graduate degree, 92 percent would allow the communist to speak. The most educated Americans are almost 50 percentage points more likely than the least educated to support free-speech rights.

Education has a powerful influence on Americans' valuation of this free-speech right and, as we shall see, on other free-speech rights as well.

Given the powerful effect that education has on Americans' willingness to value free speech, maybe the reason teachers are more likely than Americans in general to support the communist's right to speak is simply that they have more education than the average American.

In 2012, for example, 82 percent of American pre-K, elementary-, and secondary-school teachers had earned a bachelor's degree or higher, while only about one-quarter of the nonteachers had done so.

So, perhaps there is nothing inherent about teaching and teachers that makes them more supportive of free speech. It is just that they are better educated and people with more education tend to be more supportive of

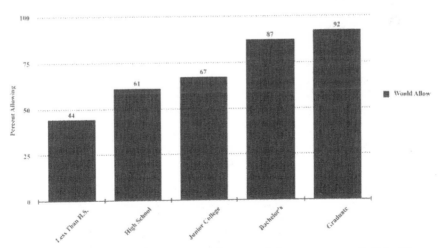

Figure 6.1. "Would you allow a communist to speak in your community?" by Educational Attainment (1972–2012)
Source: National Opinion Research Center, GSS, via the University of California at Berkeley, http://sda. berkeley.edu/cgi-bin/hsda?harcsda+gss12.

free speech. Were it not for their relatively high levels of education, in other words, teachers would be no more likely than other Americans to support the free-speech rights of a communist.

We can test this idea that teachers are more supportive of free speech only because they are better educated and not because there is something unique to teachers and teaching that makes them so. We can do this by comparing teachers with nonteachers who have as much education as they do.

Most teachers have at least a bachelor's degree. If they are more supportive of free speech only because they tend to have a higher level of education than nonteachers, we should see no difference between them and equally well-educated Americans—those with bachelor's or graduate degrees.

TEACHER CONSERVATISM

Table 6.2 compares teachers with three groups of Americans: those with a high-school diploma or less, those with junior-college degrees, and, finally, those holding a bachelor's degree or higher.

We see from the table that when compared to Americans with a high-school education or less, teachers tend to be more liberal on this free-

Table 6.2. Would you allow a communist to speak in your local community?

Teachers tend to be more liberal on free speech than Americans who have less education than they have but more conservative than Americans who have comparable levels of education—bachelor's degrees or higher. While 89 percent of nonteachers with bachelor's degrees or higher would allow a communist to speak, only 79 percent of teachers would.

	Teachers	High School or Less	Junior College	Bachelor's+
Allow	79	57	67	89
Not Allow	21	43	33	<u>11</u>
Total	100%	100%	100%	100%
(N)	(980)	(23,941)	(1,666)	(5,010)

Note: Column variable treated as independent. Percentage differences significant, p = .00; Variables used in analysis: "SPKCOM," "TEACHERS," and "DEGREE."

Source: General Social Survey, 1972–2012 via the Computer Assisted Survey Methods Program at the University of California–Berkeley.

speech issue. They tend to be more liberal as well, though only slightly so, when compared with Americans having a junior college degree. However, compared to Americans with levels of education comparable to their own—those holding a bachelor's degree or higher—teachers are not equally liberal but are instead *less* liberal. When it comes to the free-speech rights of a communist, the data are telling us that teachers are more liberal than Americans having less education than they have but more conservative than Americans with comparable levels of education.

Table 6.2 is telling us that teachers are more supportive of free speech than Americans having less education than they have but less so than Americans with comparable levels of education.

Now, when we turn to the free-speech rights of the atheist, racist, or homosexual, we find the same pattern: teachers tend to be more liberal than Americans with less education but more conservative than Americans having the most education (figure 6.2).

Table 6.2 and figure 6.2 suggest that teachers are more progressive on free speech than Americans with less than four years of college but more conservative than Americans with bachelor's degrees or higher. Education appears to have a liberalizing influence on Americans in general but it seems to have less of an effect on teachers. In relation to other Americans, our elementary- and secondary-school teachers are at once progressive and conservative.

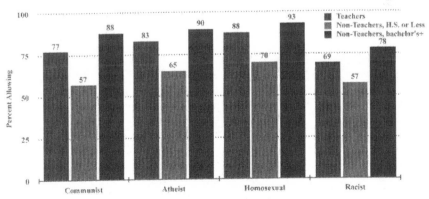

Figure 6.2. **"Would you allow a communist (atheist/homosexual/racist) to speak in your community?" by Teachers and Non-Teachers by Education (1972–2012)**
Source: National Opinion Research Center, GSS, via the University of California at Berkeley, http://sda.berkeley.edu/cgi-bin/hsda?harcsda+gss12.

Creating a Free-Speech Scale

We would like to find out more about this finding that teachers appear to be simultaneously liberal and conservative. Is it real, or is it merely an artifact of some other factor such as gender, class, religious commitment, regionalism, or the like?

To address this question, we need to streamline our analysis a bit by combining into one measure how Americans feel about the free-speech rights of our four controversial speakers: a communist, atheist, homosexual, and racist. Recall that on the GSS, Americans were not only asked if they would allow a communist, atheist, racist, or homosexual to speak in their communities but they were also asked if they would allow each of them to teach at a local college and to have a book they had written be in the public library. So, for each of the four controversial types Americans can have three responses, one for speaking, one for teaching, and one for having a book in the library, a total of 12 free-speech questions or responses in all.

To combine the responses that each American interviewed gave to the 12 free-speech questions into a single free-speech measure, let us say that every time someone gives a response that is supportive of a free-speech right—whether it be speaking, publishing, or teaching—we give them a score of "1." Every time they give a response that is not supportive of a free-speech right, we give them a score of "0."

So, for the communist, for example, with this score sheet we could conceivably have some people in our sample who would score 0, meaning they would not allow him or her to speak, publish, or teach. At the other extreme, we could have other respondents who would score a 3, meaning they would allow the communist all three of his or her rights.

We could do the same thing for the atheist, homosexual, and racist. The result is that an American who would allow all four types to speak, teach, and have their book in a library would score 3 points for each of the four types for a total score of "12," meaning that they would be highly supportive of free speech, indeed, as supportive of free speech as our scale would allow. On the other hand, someone who would deny all four types their right to speak, teach, or have their book in the library would score a "0," and would be the least supportive possible on our scale.

When we apply this free-speech score card to the combined sample of Americans in our GSS surveys, we get the results shown in table 6.3. The table includes all of the respondents from surveys administered from 1976–2012, 26,343 people in all. We can see from the table that 35 percent of the 26,343 Americans in our combined sample scored an "11" or "12" on the free-speech scale, a high score that we can interpret as meaning that they would grant communists, atheists, homosexuals, and racists most if not all of their free-speech rights. At the other extreme, however, we can see that 6 percent of our sample, 1,539 people, scored a "0," meaning that they would grant none of our four controversial types any of their free-speech rights. We can also see from table 6.3 that "9" is the median score on the scale, meaning that half of the Americans interviewed scored below "9" and half scored above it.

Given that "9" is the median score that Americans have obtained when measured on our free-speech scale, let us say that anyone who scores a

Table 6.3. Distribution of Scores on 12-point Free-speech Scale (1976–2012)

	Free-Speech Score	# of Respondents	Percent of Total Sample
	0	1,539	6
	1	944	4
	2	946	4
	3	1,378	5
	4	1,339	5
	5	1,402	5
	6	1,558	6
	7	1,512	6
	8	2,055	8
	9	2,315	9
	10	2,175	8
	11	2,590	10
	12	6,590	25
	Total	26,343	100.0%
Mean	7.8		
Median	9		
Mode	12		
Std Dev.	3.87		

Note: Variable in the analysis: FREESPEECH, a constructed variable.

Source: General Social Survey, 1976–2012 via the Computer Assisted Methods Program, the University of California–Berkeley, sda.berkeley.edu/cgi-bin/hsda?harcsda+gss10.

"10" or above on the scale may be considered "highly" supportive of free speech. Anyone who scores between "5" and "9" we will say is "moderately" supportive, and, lastly, anyone who scores a "4" or below will be considered "least" supportive.

Using these cut-off scores, we can see how Americans in general and teachers in particular have done over the last four decades on free-speech issues as we have defined them in terms of allowing a communist, atheist, homosexual, and racist their right to speak in public, teach in a local college, and have their books in the local library. Figure 6.3 shows the results.

From figure 6.3 we can see, first, that the proportion of teachers and college-educated nonteachers who are highly supportive of free speech has not changed much since the 1970s, but the percentage of the least-educated American has. While the proportion of teachers and college-educated Americans changed little if any from the 1970s to the most recent decade, Americans with a high-school education or less have grown proportionately more supportive of free speech, going from 27 percent in the 1970s to 40 percent by the 2000s, a 48 percent increase.

Second, while teachers, as a group, have been more supportive of free speech than the least educated Americans, they have been less so than nonteachers with comparable levels of education. In other words, they

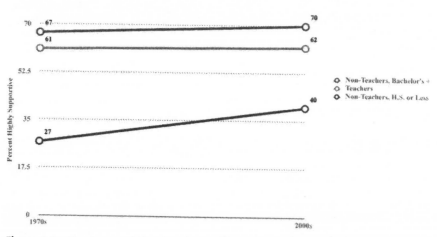

Figure 6.3. Teachers and Non-Teachers Highly Supportive of Free Speech by Educational Level by Decade.
Source: National Opinion Research Center, GSS (1972–2012), via the University of California at Berkeley.

have been more conservative than college-educated nonteachers on matters of free speech but more progressive than the least educated.

Why have teachers straddled the middle between the most highly educated and the least-educated of Americans on the matter of free speech? We can understand, given their relatively high levels of education, and the correlation between education and free speech, why they would be more supportive than Americans with less education than they have, but why would they be less supportive than comparably educated Americans? We would expect their support level to be the same as that of highly educated nonteachers, not less.

Teacher Conservatism and Gender

Perhaps teachers' conservatism is related to gender. As we have already seen, three-fourths of America's school teachers are women. Perhaps women differ from men in their support of free speech. If so, teacher conservatism may turn out to be nothing more than an artifact of gender, and has nothing to do with teachers or teaching per se; that is, contrary to what Dan Lortie and others have found, teacher conservatism has nothing to do with the occupation or anything unique about the profession.

We can test this hypothesis by simply comparing women teachers to women nonteachers who hold a bachelor's degree or higher. If the teacher conservatism we have been seeing is really the result of gender differences and not something specific to teachers or teaching as a profession or occupation, we should find no difference between women teachers and highly educated women nonteachers.

When we control for gender, we still find the familiar pattern: teachers straddle the middle. Female teachers are more liberal on free speech than female nonteachers with less than a bachelor's degree (62 vs. 37 percent highly supportive) and more conservative than female nonteachers holding a bachelor's degree or higher (62 vs. 69 percent).

Moreover, when we run the same analysis for male teachers, we also find a similar result: male teachers tend to be more liberal than the least-educated males in the population (66 vs. 42 percent highly supportive) and more conservative (66 vs. 72 percent) than the best-educated males, and these results for men are statistically significant as well. Teacher conservatism does not appear to be a result of gender.

Teacher Conservatism and Social Class

Social scientists have long been interested in the effects of social class on one's beliefs as well as on how one's beliefs affect social class.[6] While it is true that teachers are often said to be underpaid, and this in fact may be the case for the role they play in society, their average income, as we have already seen, is above the average income earned by nonteachers with comparable levels of education.[7] Is teacher conservatism vis-à-vis other well-educated Americans somehow a function of social class?

When we do this analysis we find that teachers, as a group, are still more conservative on free speech than nonteachers who make as much or more than teachers. About 75 percent of middle-class nonteachers are highly supportive of free speech, whereas only 65 percent of the teachers are.

Teacher Conservatism and Race

Race is another variable that always figures prominently in social analysis. We saw in chapter 1 that 9 percent of the American teaching cadre consists of African Americans. Is there some kind of race effect on teacher conservatism? In other words, on free-speech issues, are whites more conservative than blacks or vice-versa? Figure 6.4 suggests that race is not the reason for teacher conservatism. Both white and black teachers

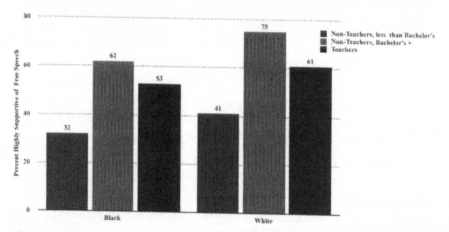

Figure 6.4. Teachers and Non-Teachers Highly Supportive of Free Speech by Education by Race.
Source: National Opinion Research Center, GSS (1972–2012), via the University of California at Berkeley.

are more conservative than their comparably educated counterparts. Race, therefore, does not appear to be responsible for teacher conservatism.

Teacher Conservatism and Religion

Teachers, as we saw in chapter 4, tend to be more religious than most nonteachers. One reason we know this is because they attend church more often. If we combine the surveys from 2000 to 2012, for example, we find that 36 percent of teachers say they attend church services one or more times per week, whereas only 26 percent of comparably educated Americans say this; teachers are 10 percentage points more likely to attend church than nonteachers of equal educational levels. Teachers, as a group, tend to be more religious than nonteachers.

When we control for church attendance, however, we still find that teachers tend to be more conservative on the free-speech issue than other well-educated Americans. Even among the teachers and nonteachers who say they never or seldom go to church, we find that teachers are more conservative. This also tends to be the case for teachers and nonteachers who say they go to church one or more times per week. Teachers are more conservative on free-speech issues than other highly educated Americans no matter whether these nonteachers almost never to go church or whether they go all of the time. Religion, then, does not seem to explain teacher conservatism.

Teacher Conservatism and Regionalism

Even if one has little interest in or knowledge of American history, one only has to watch Ken Burns' *The Civil War* to get a sense of the cultural differences that once separated the North and the South in the United States, differences that still linger, albeit in muted form, and still today distinguish them even if they no longer separate these two parts of our nation. These differences are both subtle and obvious but are often summed up by the oft-heard saying that the South is more culturally conservative than the North.

For example, corporal punishment, typically associated with conservatism, has been banned in public schools throughout the United States save for, most notably, the Southern states. Is Southern conservatism responsible for the teacher conservatism that we are seeing in the data on free speech? Do teachers appear to be more conservative than other comparably educated Americans simply because many of them are from the South and teachers in the South tend themselves to be more conservative?

The U.S. Census Bureau breaks the country down into four large census regions: Northeast, Midwest, South, and West. The South consists of the South Atlantic states (Delaware, D.C., Florida, Georgia, Maryland, North Carolina, South Carolina, Virginia, and West Virginia), the East South Central states (Alabama, Kentucky, Mississippi, and Tennessee), and the West South Central (Arkansas, Louisiana, Oklahoma, and Texas). When we analyze teachers' values among teachers in the Southern states only, we still find teachers to be conservative on free speech. For example, where 68 percent of college-educated nonteachers highly support free speech, only 61 percent of teachers do, a small but nonetheless statistically significant difference. Regionalism, too, does not seem to be the main factor in teacher conservatism.

Teacher Conservatism among Elementary-versus High-School Teachers

Now, in all of our analyses to this point we have combined elementary and secondary teachers, but some readers may suppose that there might be a difference between how these two groups view and value free speech. Some might think that elementary teachers are more conservative than secondary teachers on the issue, and that secondary-school teachers are likely to be more liberal than college-educated nonteachers.

When we do the analysis, however, we find this not to be the case. There is no significant difference between elementary- and secondary-school teachers on the issue of free speech, and both groups are more conservative than college-educated nonteachers.

Regression Analysis

Now, we can combine the variables we have just discussed into a single analysis with the use of regression, and when we do this we find that teachers still tend to be less highly supportive of free speech than nonteachers (see table A6.1 in the Appendix).

POINTS TO REMEMBER

- Among the various freedoms believed to be essential to human rights, freedom of speech has been fundamental.
- The data we have on free speech indicates that teachers are at once liberal and conservative. They are more liberal than nonteachers with less education than they have, but are more conservative than college-educated nonteachers.
- While it is possible to point to the liberalizing effects of education to explain their liberalism when compared to the least-educated of Americans, the education factor cannot explain their conservatism when compared to the best-educated Americans. Something else must be at work, otherwise the values of teachers on the free-speech issue should be similar to those of comparably educated nonteachers.
- Previous research on teaching and teachers has noted that the occupation reinforces conservative tendencies in teachers. The data suggest that teacher conservatism on free speech may be a result of broader cultural factors, their influence on children, and teachers' response to the effects that the culture has on children's understanding of freedom.

NOTES

1. See Dan C. Lortie, *Schoolteacher* (Chicago: University of Chicago Press, 1975) and Larry Cuban, *Hugging the Middle: How Teachers Teach in an Era of Accountability and Testing* (New York: Teachers College Press, 2009).

2. Betty Kenp, *King and Commons* (New York: St. Martin's Press, 1957).

3. United Nations, *Universal Declaration of Human Rights*, 2012, www.un.org/Overview/rights.html; and U.S. National Archives and Records Administration, *The U.S. Constitution—Bill of Rights*, www.archives.gov/exhibits/charters/constitution_transcript.html.

4. Hugh Lofting, *The Story of Dr. Dolittle* (New York: William Morrow, 1997).

5. John Dewey, *Democracy and Education* (New York: Free Press, 1916).

6. See, for example, Karl Marx, *Karl Marx: Selected Writings*, 2nd ed., ed. David McLellan (Oxford: University Press, 2000); Karl Mannheim, *Ideology and Utopia* (London: Routledge, 1936); Max Weber, *The Protestant Ethic and the Spirit of Capitalism*, trans. Talcott Parsons, ed. Anthony Giddens (London:

Routledge, [1904–1905] 1992); and Sung Ho Kim, "Max Weber," in Edward N. Zalta, ed., *The Stanford Encyclopedia of Philosophy*, 2012, plato.stanford.edu/ archives/fall2012/entries/weber/.

7. U.S. Census Bureau, American Community Survey, "Detailed Occupation by Median Earnings in the Past 12 Months (in 2010 Inflation-Adjusted Dollars) for the Full-Time, Year-Round Civilian Employed Population 16 Years and Over," 2006–2010 ACS 5-Year Estimates, factfinder2.census.gov/faces/tableservices/ jsf/pages/productview.xhtml?pid=ACS_10_5YR_B24121&prodType=table.

Chapter Seven

Equality

Do elementary- and secondary-school teachers, as a group, value equality any more or less than other Americans?

The value of equality is an essential component of a democratic society. The challenge of all democratic educational systems is to develop in people the foundations of equality: the tastes, dispositions, and sentiments that enable them to value equality.

While equality may be more of an ideal than a reality in many democratic systems, it nonetheless still functions as a core organizing principle in all democracies. If the Occupy Movement—regardless of its origin, effects, or eventual outcome—has demonstrated anything, it has shown us just how seriously citizens of a democracy take equality to be. If democracies live by equality, they can also die by it. They cannot, on the one hand, use the ideal of equality as a major source of legitimacy and, on the other, expect their citizens to tolerate ever-growing inequality.

Our elementary- and secondary-school teachers, whether they realize it or not, transmit the foundations of equality from one generation to the next. As we have already noted, teachers teach values not only consciously, but also unconsciously, through their example and by how they teach. Because equality is always an important measure of democracy, and therefore something with which we want to inform our children's judgment, it is natural to wonder whether our teachers value equality any more or less than other Americans.

THE MEANING OF EQUALITY

There are different kinds of equality; equality applies to different things. Scholars usually distinguish between moral equality, legal/civil rights equality, political equality, social equality, and economic equality.[1] Of these, moral equality seems to be the least controversial, and most widely accepted. It is usually interpreted to mean treating all people as equals, that is, with equal concern and respect. This is not to be confused with treating all people equally, an implausible principle.[2]

The most controversial spheres of equality are the social and the economic. "The main controversy here is whether, and if so to what extent, the state should establish far-reaching equality of social conditions for all through political measures such as redistribution of income and property, tax reform, a more equal educational system, social insurance, and positive discrimination."[3]

In the following sections we will examine teachers' views on economic equality, moral equality, and social equality.

ECONOMIC EQUALITY

Equality of Opportunity versus Equality of Outcomes

We should distinguish at the outset between two types of economic equality: (1) equality of outcome and (2) equality of opportunity. When equality of outcomes is of main concern, the principal aim is to minimize gaps in income and wealth between the rich and the poor. When equality of opportunity is the ruling principle, large gaps in income and wealth between the rich and the poor may be tolerated so long as people believe that the poor have a fair chance to get ahead if they want to, and their doing so doesn't take anything away from the rich.[4]

This latter condition depends, of course, on strong economic growth of the country as a whole. An emphasis on opportunity might well focus attention on education and how access to education can be increased. An emphasis on outcomes, however, might result in redistribution of wealth through changes in tax policy.

Consider, for example, the income inequalities in the United States in 2008, the year the U.S. fiscal crisis officially began. The median annual salary was a little over $37,000. For teachers, the average was about $52,000.[5] Total compensation for Aubrey McClendon, Chesapeake Energy's CEO was $112,464,517. Admittedly, his case was unusual. The average for CEOs that year was closer to $8 million.[6]

Believers in equality of outcome would likely find these big differences in incomes to be unacceptable, and would probably argue for higher taxes on the wealthy. Believers in equality of opportunity, on the other hand, might argue for greater access to education so that others could obtain the skills necessary for them to compete for similar high-paying positions, or they might make a case for lower taxes on small business so that they might grow and become more profitable.

Now, Americans in general have traditionally favored equality of opportunity over equality of outcome. In a 2011 Gallup poll, for example, 70 percent of Americans said that it was either extremely important or very important that the federal government act to increase equality of opportunity. In contrast, only 46 percent said the same about reducing the income and wealth gap.[7] This suggests that Americans are more inclined to endorse equality of opportunity over outcome.

The Gallup results are consistent with an earlier GSS survey taken in 1993, when Americans were then asked whether they preferred for the country to promote equal opportunity for all, allowing everyone to compete for jobs and wealth on a fair and even basis, or whether they wanted equal outcomes whereby America ensured that everyone had a decent standard of living and there were only small differences in income between the top and bottom in society. Eighty-seven percent said that they preferred equal opportunity.

In this same poll, teachers, as a group, tended, as the majority of Americans, to prefer equality of opportunity over equality of outcome but as we shall see in the next section, while they may believe in equality of opportunity, they also believe that the government should act to reduce income differences.

Should The Government Reduce Income Differences?

Controversy over equality is often about the government's role in reducing inequality. One of the most basic questions is whether and how much the government should try to reduce income differences and, if it should try, what measures it should take. Should, for example, the government reduce income differences between the rich and poor by, say, raising taxes on the wealthy or giving assistance to the poor, or should it not be concerned with income differences?

Where have teachers come down on this issue? When all is said and done, teachers, as a group, tend to support government action to reduce income differences.

Teachers' position on this issue is at first hard to see because they tend to make more money than the average American and income tends to be negatively correlated with support for government action; the higher Americans' incomes, the less likely they are to support government action to reduce income differences.

It also happens that regionalism makes a difference for how Americans feel about this issue. Southerners tend to oppose government action, and many teachers live in the South. But when we control for income and regionalism, we see that teachers, as a group, tend to support government action to reduce income differences (see table A7.1 in Appendix A).

Should Government Help the Poor or Should the Poor Help Themselves?

Elementary- and secondary-school teachers have also been inclined to believe that the government has a responsibility to improve the standard of living of all poor Americans, though the percentage believing this has declined over the last four decades, suggesting that, as a group, teachers have felt more strongly the rise of conservatism in America, and that it has had a greater impact on their beliefs than it has on other, comparably educated Americans.

In the 1970s, for example, about 55 percent of teachers said that the government should do everything possible to improve the standard of living of all poor Americans. By the 2000s, however, teachers, as a group, had grown more conservative on the issue. By then only about one-quarter of them held this view. By the 2000s, moreover, teachers were no more likely than other highly educated Americans to believe that the government should intervene on behalf of the poor.

ECONOMIC EQUALITY

It seems reasonable to suppose that people who have themselves experienced economic equality would be more likely to value economic equality. So, to what degree have teachers experienced economic equality?

Recall that in chapter 1 we noted that the average annual salary for U.S. teachers as of 2010 was between $47,000 and $51,000 per year, close to the $51,000 per year that persons with bachelor's degrees averaged. So, by this measure, teachers' compensation appears to be in line with that of other Americans. However, table 7.1 shows that only about 3 percent of teachers make more than $75,000 per year where almost one-third of nonteachers with similar educations do. So, by this measure, teachers' opportunity are limited in so far as they are able to be in the upper third of income earners with their educational levels, that is, they are subject to income inequality.

Now, one of the main conclusions reached from the data presented here is that teachers make an enormous but "silent" contribution to a society's basic stability and development by the values that they hold and convey to children. Teachers, as we have said elsewhere, play a unique role as values governors, keeping some values from being taken to excess and enhancing others. But their contribution is "silent" in the sense that most

Table 7.1. How Much Do Teachers Make Compared to Other Highly Educated Americans?

From 2006 to 2010, over half of America's school teachers reported annual incomes between $40k and $75k. They were, however, 28 percentage points *less* likely than comparably educated Americans to make over $75k.

Annual Income	Teachers with BA/BS Degrees or Higher	Nonteachers with BA/BS Degrees or Higher
$1,000 to $39,999	43%	36%
$40,000 to $74,999	54%	33%
$75,000 +	3%	31%
Total	100%	100%
(N)	(178)	(1,385)

Note: Percentage differences significant at p<.01 level. Variables used in the analysis: RINCOM06, TEACHERS, and DEGREE.

Source: National Opinion Research Center, General Social Survey, via the Computer Assisted Survey Methods Program at the University of California–Berkeley. Surveys are from 2006–2010.

if not all of our attention these days is focused on their impact on student achievement and high-stakes testing.

Teachers' impact on students' values and, through them, on the stability of society as a whole has received little serious attention, probably because it is so difficult to conceptualize and measure, a challenge that the present work has taken up, albeit in a modest way.

How much is teachers' contribution to social stability worth? The calculation of the economic value of teachers' work in this regard exceeds the scope of the present work. But those who are interested in figuring out these sorts of things should do so. Too much is at stake to ignore it.

MORAL EQUALITY

How can we measure whether or not Americans in general and teachers in particular value moral equality? Moral equality seems to involve at least a basic disposition to feel concern and respect for others.[8] In other words, a society in which the ideal of moral equality is taken seriously and used by its members to guide their behavior toward others should be one in which people tend to be considerate of all others without regard to race, class, gender, and the other criteria of discrimination. In such a moral commonwealth, there should be, more often than not, thoughtful and sympathetic regard for all, not just some. Presumably, such a society would also generally be a caring society.[9]

On the first ingredient of moral equality—a basic sense of concern and respect—we can take some direction from James Q. Wilson's *The Moral Sense* in which he argued that sympathy, fairness, and self-control are essential components of moral behavior and the moral sense.[10] Are teachers more or less sympathetic than other Americans?

Individualism

The tendency of capitalist democracies to foster extreme forms of individualism has long been a theme and concern in studies of democratic societies.[11] There are different understandings of individualism. Alexis de Tocqueville believed it to be the disposition to care only about oneself, one's family and one's small little circle of friends, and to be indifferent to everyone and everything else beyond them.

A more popular understanding of individualism is the belief that people should "stand on their own two feet," or learn how to take care of themselves and not depend on others, a notion that implies some of what Tocqueville meant. Given this commonsense notion of individualism, teachers appear to be less prone than other Americans to be hyperindividualistic.

In the 2002 and 2004 surveys, for example, Americans were asked whether they agreed or disagreed whether "those in need have to learn to take care of themselves and not depend on others." About 53 percent of Americans believed that those in need should take care of themselves and not depend on others while only 35 percent of teachers believed this. A greater proportion of teachers, in other words, tended to disagree with the statement, suggesting that they were less prone to let people fend for themselves and, accordingly, less individualistic in this sense, than other Americans.

Compassion

Compassion was a major theme in the administration of George W. Bush, though the pressure to talk about compassion had been building from the Reagan era on. Republicans' interest in compassion has been based, at least in part, on their concern to reduce the role of government.

A reduction-of-government agenda gives rise to the practical problem that some government interventions specifically target the poor and to eliminate these programs is to risk being, or at least appearing to be, calloused or indifferent with regard to suffering and distress of others. An emphasis on "compassion" addressed this political problem and at the same time recognized people's natural tendency to sympathize with the misery and grief of others and to act on these sentiments.

Whatever their political persuasion, teachers' beliefs have tended to be more compassionate than those of less educated nonteachers but no more so than comparably educated Americans. In other words, when it comes to compassion, the level of one's education seems to be the major factor.

Table 7.2 lists four "compassion" questions that we can combine into a single measure of compassion, creating in effect a compassion scale. The scale runs from 6 to 25, with 6 being the lowest possible score and 25 the highest. The median or mid-score is 17. Using this scale, teachers, as a group, were 9 percentage points more likely to score high than non-

Table 7.2. Measures of Compassion and Items in Compassion Scale

1. Sometimes I don't feel very sorry for other people when they are having problems.
2. Other people's misfortunes do not usually disturb me a great deal.
3. Those in need have to learn how to take care of themselves and not depend on others.
4. Personally assisting people in trouble is very important to me.

Note: Names of variables are: "empathy2," "empathy4," "careself," "selffrst," and "peoptrbl."

Source: University of California–Berkeley, *Computer-Assisted Survey Methods Program: The GSS Cumulative Data File 1972–2004.*

teachers with high-school educations or less. There was not, however, any significant difference between teachers and highly educated nonteachers.

Little Acts of Compassion

Of course, saying is one thing and doing is another. We are interested in compassion not just as opinions but as actions; when it comes to compassion, acts count more than opinions.

Do American teachers perform acts of compassion more than other Americans?

There are some questions on our survey that help us to get at actions versus words. These questions ask people to say how many times within the last week, month, or year they have done things such as given blood, given food or money to a homeless person, returned excess change given them by mistake, let someone cut ahead of them in line, do volunteer work for or give money to a charity, give up their seat to a stranger, helped carry a stranger's belongings, let someone borrow an item, looked after a plant or pet while someone was away, and gave directions to a stranger.

The question for our purposes is whether teachers perform these little acts of compassion more than nonteachers.

Table 7.3 is a list of seven little acts of compassion. In the 2002 and 2004 surveys, Americans were asked how frequently they did these things within the past year. When can add these seven acts of compassion together, creating a single "compassion" scale. Then, when we use this scale to compare teachers with nonteachers we find that teachers are about 10 percentage points more likely than other Americans to engage in little acts of compassion; that is, they are, as a group and by these measures, a little more compassionate (table 7.4).

Table 7.3. Seven Questions to Measure Little Acts of Compassion

During the past 12 months, how often have you done each of the following things:
1. *Given directions to a stranger?*
2. *Offered your seat on a bus or in a public place to a stranger?*
3. *Allowed a stranger to go ahead of you in line?*
4. *Carried a stranger's belongings, like groceries, a suitcase, or shopping bags?*
5. *Looked after a person's plants, mail, or pets while they were away?*
6. *Given money to a charity?*
7. *Give money to homeless person?*

Why do teachers, by these measures, seem to be a little more compassionate than other Americans? As it turns out, teachers' compassion does not have anything to do with their teaching per se. It is rather linked to their education levels. Their education appears to be the key factor in their level of compassion and not anything in particular about their being a teacher.

SOCIAL EQUALITY

Social equality has to do with one's social status or ranking in society, one's relative position or rank in the hierarchy of prestige or in the eyes of others. As the German sociologist Max Weber pointed out, social status is linked to other things—money and influence being two important ones—and, accordingly, most people are concerned to increase or raise their social status.

This is particularly true of young people living in democratic societies which, by virtue of their emphasis on freedom, promise a better life. In

Table 7.4. High Scores on Compassion Scale by Teachers and Nonteachers (2002–2004)

	Teachers	Nonteachers
Low Compassion	40	51
High Compassion	60	49
Total	100%	100%
N	(88)	(2,568)

Note: Variables used in the analysis: COMPASSION and TEACHERS; p = 0.00.

Source: General Social Survey via the Computer Methods Program, the University of California–Berkeley, sda.berkeley.edu/cgi-bin/hsda?harcsda+gss10. Data from 2000–2004.

comparison to older, traditional societies, people in a democracy are freer to do and be what they want. The constraints of family, community, and church are attenuated and no longer have the hold they once did. People see opportunity to pursue different careers and lifestyles, and generally to improve their lot by being socially mobile.

Social mobility, then, is related to the belief in equality of opportunity. The more people believe in the existence of equal opportunity, the harder they will strive to be upwardly mobile. The more upwardly mobile they are, in turn, the more they will believe in equal opportunity. Both the fact and the belief need to be present if the value of opportunity is to be sustained over time. Inequality and high unemployment undermine faith in equal opportunity and are, of course, main factors behind the Occupy Movement.

Now, teachers would be more likely to convey the value of opportunity to their students if they themselves were upwardly mobile and had therefore personally experienced opportunity. So, we would like to know whether teachers, as a group, have been upwardly mobile. Have they, in fact, done better than their parents, and have they done so more than other Americans?

Teachers' Educational Opportunity/Mobility

Just as there are different kinds of equality, so also are there different kinds of equality of opportunity, and educational opportunity is one of the most important of these. We can get at least a rough idea of teachers' educational opportunity by comparing their educational mobility with other Americans.

By "educational mobility" we mean here the difference between the educational attainment of teachers as compared to that of their parents, particularly their fathers. Americans in general and teachers in particular who have achieved higher levels of education than their fathers are considered to have been upwardly mobile in terms of their education.

What percentage of the nation's teachers, for example, had fathers who earned only a high-school diploma or even did not finish high school? Teachers, remember, as compared to Americans in general, have high levels of education.

In the 1970s, 81 percent of teachers had fathers with only high-school educations or less while only 74 percent of the fathers of nonteachers had this little education. By the 2000s, the percent of teachers who had fathers with high-school educations or less had dropped to 69 percent but so had the figure for nonteachers. It had dropped to 59 percent. In each of the last four decades, then, proportionately more teachers than nonteachers had fathers with low educations. In other words, in so far as education is concerned, teachers have been, as a group, more upwardly mobile than nonteachers.

Race and Educational Mobility among Teachers

If the teaching profession has been good to teachers in general, it has been particularly good to African American teachers, for no less than 90 percent of them have themselves obtained a four-year degree or more while their fathers managed to get only high-school diplomas or less. Teaching, then, appears to have provided significant educational opportunity for both American whites and blacks, but even more for blacks.

POINTS TO REMEMBER

- Teachers, as a group, tend to favor government action to reduce income differences between the rich and the poor.
- Like other highly educated Americans, teachers believe that the government should help the poor as opposed to leaving the poor to fend for themselves, but the percentage of teachers who hold this view has halved over the last four decades, dropping from 55 percent in the 1970s to 25 percent in the 2000s.

NOTES

1. Stephan Gosepath, "Equality," in Edward N. Zalta, ed., *The Stanford Encyclopedia of Philosophy*, Spring 2011, plato.stanford.edu/archives/win2005/entries/equality.

2. Ronald R. Dworkin, *Taking Rights Seriously* (Cambridge, MA: Harvard University Press, 1977).

3. Gosepath, "Equality," chap. 5.

4. Sidney Verba and Gary R. Orren, "The Meaning of Equality in America," *Political Science Quarterly* 3 (1985): 369–87.

5. See "Rankings and Estimates," National Education Association, www.nea.org/assets/docs/HE/09rankings.pdf.

6. Mike Winfroath, "CEO Pay Dives in a Rough 2008," *USA Today*, May 8, 2009, usatoday30.usatoday.com/money/companies/management/2009-05-01-ceo-pay-for-2008-falls_N.htm.

7. Frank Newport, "Americans Prioritize Economy over Reducing Wealth Gap," Gallup, Inc., www.gallup.com/poll/151568/Americans-Prioritize-Growing-Economy-Reducing-Wealth-Gap.aspx.

8. Dworkin, *Taking Rights Seriously*.

9. On these points see Philip Selznick, *The Moral Commonwealth* (Berkeley: University of California Press, 1992) and Nell Noddings, *Caring: A Feminine Approach to Ethics and Moral Education* (Berkeley: University of California Press, 1984).

10. James Q. Wilson, *The Moral Sense* (New York: Free Press, 1993).

11. Robert N. Bellah, Richard Madsen, William M. Sullivan, Ann Swidler, and Steven M. Tipton, *Habits of the Heart: Individualism and Commitment in American Life* (Berkeley: University of California Press, 1985); Seymour Martin Lipset, *American Exceptionalism: A Double-Edged Sword* (New York: Norton, 1996); Alexis de Tocqueville, *Democracy in America* (New York: Doubleday, 1969).

Chapter Eight

Science

Do teachers value science more than other Americans? Do they tend to know more about science than nonteachers, particularly nonteachers who have comparable levels of education? These questions are important because we must assume that teachers' appreciation and knowledge of science influences their students' appreciation and knowledge of it.

One of the best measures that we have for how much students know about science compared to students from other countries is the Program for International Student Assessment, otherwise known as the PISA test.[1]

This test is developed and administered by the United Nation's Organization for Economic Cooperation and Development (OECD). PISA is designed to measure how much 15-year-olds know about science. With PISA, we can compare how well our children do with the performance of students from both OECD and non-OECD countries.

The OECD countries include: Australia, Austria, Belgium, Canada, Chile, Czech Republic, Denmark, Estonia, Finland, France, Germany, Greece, Hungary, Iceland, Ireland, Israel, Italy, Japan, Korea, Republic of Luxembourg, Mexico, the Netherlands, New Zealand, Norway, Poland, Portugal, Slovak Republic, Slovenia, Spain, Sweden, Switzerland, Turkey, the United Kingdom, and the United States.

The non-OECD countries include the following: Albania, Argentina, Azerbaijan, Brazil, Bulgaria, Chinese Taipei, Colombia, Croatia, Dubai–United Arab Emirates, Hong Kong–China, Indonesia, Jordan, Kazakhstan, Kyrgyz Republic, Latvia, Liechtenstein, Lithuania, Macao–China, Montenegro, Republic of, Panama, Peru, Qatar, Romania, Russian Federation, Serbia, Republic of, Shanghai–China, Singapore, Thailand, Trinidad and Tobago, Tunisia, and Uruguay.

The PISA science scale ranges from 0 to 1000. The most recent publicly available data is from 2009, and interested readers can even explore the data themselves with the International Data Explorer provided by the National Center for Education Statistics.[2]

So, how did our 15-year-olds do on the latest science test compared to kids from other countries? Our U.S. students averaged 502 on the test, just above the OECD average of 501. Among the OECD countries, Japan's students had the highest average at 539. But in addition to Japan, we trailed behind Australia, Belgium, Canada, Estonia, Finland, Germany, Hungary, Ireland, Korea, the Netherlands, New Zealand, Poland, Slovenia, Switzerland, and the United Kingdom.

The highest average science score on the PISA, however, was not Japan's or from an OECD country. It was from China, whose Shanghai students averaged 575 on the test. From the non-OECD countries we were bested by not only China's Shanghai but also Chinese Taipei, Hong Kong, Liechtenstein, Macao, and Singapore.

Needless to say, students' performance on PISA (and other international tests as well) has elicited growing concern and commentary.[3] Among the various explanations given for why U.S. students tend do less well than students from other countries is the factor of teacher quality. A number of factors no doubt figure into PISA science scores—student effort, ability, and preparation, to mention but a few. But how much their teachers know about science—what the experts call "pedagogical content knowledge"—is surely important.[4]

So, how much do American teachers know about science? We do not have anything like the PISA test to measure teachers' science knowledge. But the General Social Survey (GSS) does have some basic questions from which we can get some clues. We can separate out American teachers from the general sample to see how they compare with other Americans, particularly those having a college degree. In doing this, of course, we can only get a rough idea of teachers' knowledge of science as compared to nonteachers. But even this approximation might give us some rough idea of U.S. teachers' knowledge of basic science.

Consider, for example, the GSS question of whether the earth revolves around the sun or the sun around the earth. Here is how the interviewers put the question to Americans in the 2006, 2008, and 2010 surveys:

Now, I would like to ask you a few short questions like those you might see on a television game show. For each statement that I read, please tell me if it is true or false. If you don't know or aren't sure, just tell me so, and we will skip to the next question. Remember true, false, or don't know. . . . Now, does the Earth go around the Sun, or does the Sun go around the Earth?

It has been almost 500 years since Copernicus published his heliocentric theory of the universe and one would think that all but a small percentage of Americans would get this basic question right but about one-fifth of Americans think that the sun revolves around the earth, and about 10 percent of teachers did (table 8.1).

We expect teachers to do better on this question than nonteachers, and American teachers did. Only about 10 percent of them said that the sun revolves around the earth. Still, this is poor consolation as there are about 3.7 million teachers in the country, and if 10 percent of them say this then the conclusion we must draw is that as many as 370,000 American teachers think the earth is the center of the universe.

Now, of course, not all school teachers in America teach science. But most elementary-school teachers do, as elementary classrooms tend to be self-contained, meaning that one teacher teaches all subjects, including science.

About 70 percent of America's 3.7 million teachers are elementary-school teachers. This amounts to about 2,590,000 teachers. So, 10 percent of 2,590,000 is 259,000 elementary-school teachers, many of whom apparently think that the sun revolves around the earth. These teachers,

Table 8.1. Teachers and Nonteachers Response to the Question: "Does the Earth go around the Sun, or does the Sun go around the Earth?" (2006–2012)

	Teachers	Non-Teachers
Earth around Sun	88%	79%
Sun around Earth	12%	21%
Total	100%	100%
N =	(211)	(4,665)

Note: Variables used in the analysis are "EARTHSUN" and "TEACHERS" with the latter treated as the column variable. Percentage differences statistically significant ($X^2 = 10.05$ $p = 0.00$). Ninety-five percent confidence limits for 12% of teachers who gave wrong answer are 8–18%.

Source: National Opinion Research Center, General Social Survey (via the Computer-assisted Survey Methods Program at the University of California–Berkeley), 2006–2012 surveys combined, sda.berkeley.edu/.

moreover, are teaching American children science. Furthermore, if we assume that each of these teachers instructs about 20 children, then it is possible that more than 5 million American children are every day learning their science from teachers who do not know whether the earth revolves around the sun or vice-versa.

Lest it be thought we making too much of this one example, we can examine teachers' responses to other science questions also asked of them in the survey. Consider, for example, the question of how long it takes for the earth to revolve around the sun. Here is the exact wording of the question that the interviewer put to the respondents:

Now, I would like to ask you a few short questions like those you might see on a television game show. For each statement that I read, please tell me if it is true or false. If you don't know or aren't sure, just tell me so, and we will skip to the next question. Remember true, false, or don't know. . . . How long does it take for the Earth to go around the Sun: one day, one month, or one year?

In this case there is no significant difference between the percentage of the American population in general and of teachers in particular who get this one wrong (table 8.2). About 20 percent of both groups say that it takes something other than one year for the earth to revolve around the sun. So, in this instance, given the number of teachers in the country, it is possible that as many as 518,000 teachers who are ignorant of this basic science fact are teaching science to more than 10.3 million American students.

Table 8.2.   Teachers and Nonteachers Response to the Question: "How long does it take for the Earth to go around the Sun?" (2006–2012)

	Teachers	Non-Teachers
One Year	81%	77%
Other than One Year	19%	23%
Total	100%	100%
N =	(178)	(3,369)

Note: Variables used in the analysis are "SOLARREV" and "TEACHERS" with the latter treated as the column variable. Percentage differences not statistically significant (ChiSq = 1.32, p -.55). Ninety-five percent confidence limits for 19% of teachers who gave wrong answer are 14–25%.

Source: National Opinion Research Center, General Social Survey (via the Computer-assisted Survey Methods Program at the University of California–Berkeley), 2006, 2008, and 2010 surveys combined, sda.berkeley.edu/.

Not all of the science questions on the GSS have to do with astronomy. Another question, for example, has to do with how lasers work. In this case the interviewer asks the respondent a true-false question:

Now, I would like to ask you a few short questions like those you might see on a television game show. For each statement that I read, please tell me if it is true or false. If you don't know or aren't sure, just tell me so, and we will skip to the next question. Remember true, false, or don't know. . . . Lasers work by focusing sound waves. (Is that true or false?)

About one-third of Americans and American teachers alike get this one wrong, thinking that lasers work by focusing sound waves instead of light (table 8.3).

The pattern is similar for other questions. Another true-false question, for example, asks whether electrons are smaller than atoms and in this case about one-quarter of Americans in general and teachers in particular say that it is false that electrons are smaller than atoms.

Anywhere from 6 to 14 percent of teachers do not know that the continents were once joined but have been separating and will continue to do so. About 8 percent do not know that they center of the earth is hot. Over 20 percent believe that antibiotics kill viruses as well as bacteria. About 18 percent do not know that the father's gene decides whether the baby is a boy or girl. Over 10 percent say that the sun never shines at the South Pole.

Table 8.3. Teachers and Non-Teachers Response to the Question: "Lasers work by focusing sound waves—is that true or false?" (2006–2012)

	Teachers	Non-Teachers
True	34%	31%
False	66%	69%
Total	100%	100%
N =	(140)	(3,410)

Note: Data are from the National Opinion Research Center, General Social Survey (via the Computer-assisted Survey Methods Program at the University of California, Berkeley), 2006, 2008 and 2010 surveys combined. Variables used in the analysis are "LASERS" and "TEACHERS" with the latter treated as the column variable. Percentage differences between teachers and non-teachers are not statistically significant (ChiSq – 1.96, p = .24). 95% confidence limits for 31% of Teachers who gave wrong answer are 26–44%. Retrieved April 10, 2013 from http://sda.berkeley.edu/.

Evolution

The question on which American teachers seem to depart most dramatically from scientific knowledge, however, is the one on evolution. Here is the question:

Now, I would like to ask you a few short questions like those you might see on a television game show. For each statement that I read, please tell me if it is true or false. If you don't know or aren't sure, just tell me so, and we will skip to the next question. Remember true, false, or don't know. . . . Human beings, as we know them today, developed from earlier species of animals. (Is that true or false?)

From Table 8.4 we can see that 51 percent of nonteachers said that this was true and 59 percent of teachers did as well.

The Gallup Organization has put a similar question on evolution to Americans, and it gave respondents three scenarios from which to choose.[5] Here is the question they asked:

Which of the following comes closest to your view on the origin and development of human beings—(human beings have developed over millions of years from less advanced forms of life, but God guided this process, human beings have developed over millions of years from less advanced forms of life, but God had no part in the process (or) God created human beings pretty much in their present form at one time in the last 10,000 years or so)?

Table 8.4. Teachers and Nonteachers Response to the Question: "Human beings, as we know them today, developed from earlier species of animals—is that true or false?" (2006–2012)

	Teachers	Non-Teachers
True	59%	51%
False	41%	49%
Total	100%	100%
N=	(183)	(3,954)

Note: $X^2 = 4.61$ $p = -.05$. Variables used in the analysis are "EVOLVED" and "TEACHERS" with the latter treated as the column variable. Ninety-five percent confidence limits for the 59% of teachers who said "true" are 51–67.

Source: National Opinion Research Center, General Social Survey (via the Computer-assisted Survey Methods Program at the University of California–Berkeley), 2006, 2008, and 2010 surveys combined, sda.berkeley.edu/.

As recently as May, 2012, 46 percent of Americans selected the third option, that God created human beings about 10,000 years ago, indicating their belief in creationism. Thus, for Americans generally, the GSS and the Gallup results are much the same: about 45 percent of the U.S. population apparently believes that human kind was created about 10,000 years ago. According to the GSS, about 40 percent of teachers believe in creationism as well.

Given that there are about 3.7 million elementary- and secondary-school teachers in the United States, this amounts to almost 1.5 million teachers. Again, assuming that each teacher teaches at least 20 children in a given year (secondary-school teachers will have more), it is possible that as many as 30 million students are being taught by teachers who believe in creationism.

This is not to say, of course, that the teachers who believe in creationism espouse their beliefs in their classrooms. It is to suggest, however, that teachers who believe in creationism are probably less likely to value science and especially the scientific method. As James Tannebaum, a fourth- and fifth-grade science teacher in New York says, they do not reject science wholesale but they "cherry pick it," choosing to believe those aspects of science that do not conflict with their way of life.[6]

Science Education Systems

Debate over how U.S. students' performance in science stacks up against that of students from other countries continues as of this writing. The latest results from the Trends in International Mathematics and Science Study (TIMSS) has U.S. fourth graders tied for seventh place with three other countries, out of a total of 57 nations where the test was given.[7] U.S. eighth graders tied for 12th place with 10 other countries out of a total of 56 nations.

Part of the controversy surrounding the question of how well U.S. students perform internationally has to do with the percentage of students of poverty that are included in the comparisons. Stanford researcher Martin Carnoy has argued that when differences in countries' social-class composition is taken into account, U.S. students rank higher on international reading and math tests.[8]

In light of international tests results, a major strategy that the United States has taken to improve the performance of its students in science, as well as in other subjects, is the centralization of its curricula through the Common Core State Standards, an initiative coordinated by the National Governors' Association and the Council of Chief State School Officers.[9]

Historically, the task of education in America has been left largely to the states, and each state has developed its own system of education with its own standards and testing regime. Thus, it should come as no surprise that states vary as to their students' performance. Massachusetts students, in fact, tend to compete well with students from other countries, often scoring in the top 10.

This is not to say that there has been no uniformity in what students in the United States have had to learn. What has been taught and learned in American elementary and secondary schools has not varied so much from state to state that students have not been able to move from one system to the next.

A student going from, say, Illinois to New York does not encounter a completely alien system of education. Adjustments might be necessary. He or she might be behind or ahead in some subjects but overall things would even out relatively quickly so that the transfer student can graduate on time. But this being said, American education is still a relatively decentralized system, a fact that the Common Core has been designed to change.

The Common Core State Standards are essentially a set of statements about what it is every student should know in specific subject areas. They "define what students should understand and be able to do" and are intended "to provide teachers and parents with a common understanding of what students are expected to learn." Here is an example of a Common Core standard for Kindergarten mathematics:

> Students use numbers, including written numerals, to represent quantities and to solve quantitative problems, such as counting objects in a set; counting out a given number of objects; comparing sets or numerals; and modeling simple joining and separating situations with sets of objects, or eventually with equations such as $5 + 2 = 7$ and $7 - 2 = 5$. (Kindergarten students should see addition and subtraction equations, and student writing of equations in kindergarten is encouraged, but it is not required.) Students choose, combine, and apply effective strategies for answering quantitative questions, including quickly recognizing cardinalities of small sets of objects, counting and producing sets of given sizes, counting the number of

objects in combined sets, or counting the number of objects that remain in a set after some are taken away.

While it is true, as some have said, that science content knowledge—familiarity with basic science facts—is by no means the whole of science education, it surely must be a part of it. Knowledge of basic science facts—or lack thereof—may not be an indicator of how much a person values science but it can be taken as a clue as to how much science is valued in the society. If one or a few persons do not know that the earth revolves around the sun—this can be attributed to ignorance. If as much as one-fifth of the population does not know it—this indicates a weakness not in the individual but in the educational system as a whole.

It is still too early to say whether or not the movement to a Common Core will help U.S. students rise to the top in international science rankings. To the degree, however, that it addresses the gaps in basic science knowledge that apparently exists among too many U.S. elementary- and secondary-school teachers, it may well have a salutary impact. This, however, depends on how well it is implemented.

POINTS TO REMEMBER

- On international science tests (TIMSS) administered in 57 countries in 2011, U.S. fourth graders tied for seventh place, and eighth graders tied for 12th place.
- U.S. educators and many Americans are not satisfied with having American students' performance in science lag behind that of students from Korea, Singapore, Japan, Russia, Chinese Taipei, Finland, Hong Kong, and the United Kingdom.
- Recent research out of Stanford University claims that U.S. students' average scores in reading and mathematics are lower than those of students from other countries because they include the scores of a greater percentage of students of poverty. American students fare better when they are compared with countries with similar social-class composition.
- According to the GSS, from 6 to 20 percent of U.S. elementary- and secondary-school teachers do not know the correct answers to basic

science questions such as whether the earth revolves around the sun or vice-versa.

- Data from the combined 2006–2008 GSS surveys indicate that as much as 40 percent of American teachers subscribed to creationism, the view that God created human beings as they are today and did so about 10,000 years ago.
- In an effort to create a more standardized elementary- and secondary-school curriculum, many U.S. states have adopted the Common Core.

NOTES

1. See "Program for International Student Assessment," National Center for Education Statistics, Institute of Education Sciences, nces.ed.gov/surveys/pisa/.

2. "International Data Explorer," National Center for Education Statistics, Institute of Education Sciences, nces.ed.gov/surveys/international/ide/.

3. Sam Dillon, "Top Test Scores from Shanghai Stun Educators," *New York Times*, December 7, 2010, www.nytimes.com/2010/12/07/education/07education. html?pagewanted=all.

4. Lee S. Shulman, "Those Who Understand: Knowledge Growth in Teaching," *Educational Researcher* 15 (1986): 4–14; Betsy Becker and Ariel Aloe, "Teacher Science Knowledge and Student Science Achievement," paper presented at the annual meeting of the American Educational Research Association, 2008.

5. "In U.S., 46% Hold Creationist View of Human Origins," Gallup, Inc., www.gallup.com/poll/155003/Hold-Creationist-View-Human-Origins.aspx.

6. Jacob Tannenbaum, "Creation, Evolution and Indisputable Facts," *Scientific American* 308 (January 2013): 11.

7. "Trends in International Mathematics and Science Study," Institute of Education Sciences, National Center for Education Statistics, nces.ed.gov/timss/results11_science11.asp.

8. See Jonathan Rabinowitz, "Poor Ranking on International Test Misleading about U.S. Student Performance, Stanford Researcher Finds," Stanford Report, January 15, 2013, news.stanford.edu/news/2013/january/test-scores-ranking-011513.html.

9. "Common Core," Common Core State Standards Initiative, www.corestandards.org/.

Part III

TEACHERS' VALUES
AND DEMOCRACY

Chapter Nine

Teachers' Values
in Unsteady Democracy

The main hypothesis that arises from the analysis in the previous chapters is that teachers function as values regulators, and as such play a particularly important role in stabilizing democratic societies, which, more than traditional societies, have a tendency to grow imbalanced. Democracies, for example, tend to take self-expression and freedom to extremes while at the same time they erode important social values that are the foundation of social capital formation and community.

Teachers' values tend to counteract the negative and self-destructive aspects of democracy. Their positive effects on it are both direct and indirect. They directly affect what students learn and this, in turn, affects a democracy's capacity to grow, develop, and compete with other nations. But they also indirectly affect a democracy's capacity to maintain itself and to keep from going to self-destructive extremes. The direct effect is surely important but without the indirect effect the democracy itself is put at risk, and if it be lost, all of the value added via the learning of science, mathematics, and reading does not matter.

Thus, teachers add value not only to children's intellectual growth but to their moral development as well, and upon the second the first is no little dependent, and both are needed to support our unsteady democracies.

THE VICISSITUDES OF DEMOCRACY

Radical Individualism

One of the imbalances that Alexis de Tocqueville says that democracy tends to foster is radical individualism. More than any other type of regime, a democracy provides opportunities for personal advancement and success.

But pursuit of the widespread opportunity that democracy affords creates lifestyles that he describes as "agitated and active." There is little time left over for thinking about things beyond one's self, one's family, and one's little circle of friends. With this group formed to their taste, people are prone to forget about everything else, including and especially government, which they happily leave to others. They are radical individualists, and their individualism undermines the making of the civil society upon which a democracy depends.

Democracies also, he suggests, tend to have an "edginess" to them. People have a chance to better their lives and those of their loved ones, but there is no guarantee that they will succeed. They get "excited by the chance of success" but they are also "irritated by the thought of failure." The democratic citizen, then, tends to be impatient, preferring immediate gratification to utility over the long term.

GOING BEYOND LIBERTY'S LIMITS

The radical individualism that democracy tends to foster gets mixed with another one of democracy's characteristics—its unrelenting insistence on individual freedom—and the mix of the two encourages people to think of freedom as being able to do whatever they want, often regardless of the consequences for others.

In an advanced capitalist culture such as ours, there is great pressure to define freedom in ways consistent with and supportive of the consumption of goods and services. The idea of freedom as being allowed to do whatever one wants or buy whatever one wants (on credit) fits the (dollar) bill. However, when people's "freedom" to consume is brought up short, as it has been in our current economic crisis, their excitement at the prospects of success turns to bitterness when they encounter wage stagnation, tight credit, and even unemployment. They lose confidence in their leadership and take to the streets.

The general notion of freedom as being able to do whatever one wants, for example, is easily translated into other freedoms such as the freedom of movement—one of the basic human rights. In this instance, freedom to do what one wants becomes freedom to go where one wants when one wants. Historically, this has been a sense of freedom readily actualized for most middle-class Americans via the automobile and a well-developed highway system whereby one's movement is not limited by bus or train schedules.

Behind the bailout of the American auto industry, there were, as everyone knew, noneconomic factors at play, among which were not only national identity but also the vehicles by which, both figuratively and literally, many found a new way to express what may be a distinctly American view of freedom.

People do not come to their understanding of freedom by instinct but by education. Freedom must be learned and taught. In a democracy, particularly in a modern capitalist democracy, it is taught in a variety of ways. It is taught by parents in the home. It is taught at school. And, of course, it is taught—as we have just suggested in the case of the automobile—via the general culture, through advertising and consumption, games and recreational pursuits, social networks, and no doubt other ways as yet to be discovered.

All societies must strike some balance between freedom and self-expression on the one hand, and order and security on the other. Order and orderliness are characteristics of a society and distinguish it from a mere collection of individuals who possess nothing in common. Too much freedom brings disorder and even chaos. Too little slows growth and produces stagnation. But not all societies strike the same balance nor do they achieve balance in the same way.

Nondemocracies can and do achieve balance by relying on external force and controls—large and pervasive police forces, heavy surveillance, harsh penalties, and the like. But while tyrannies can and do achieve their order from the outside-in, democracies have to achieve theirs from the inside-out. The more a democracy has to rely for its order on external means, the less, by definition, it is a democracy. Democracies, therefore, need and want citizens who are able and willing to control themselves as opposed to having to be controlled by others.

Because democracies depend on individuals to bring order to themselves and their own lives, they must necessarily rely heavily on education. Perhaps Rousseau was correct, and people are born with a natural disposition to curb and restrain their individual wills. But they tend not to do so if their culture wants them to be individuals and encourages self-expression. In such democratic cultures, they must learn self-regulation and restraint. But they do not acquire these habits automatically. In democratic societies, freedom's limits must be taught and learned.

But no education is perfectly efficient. The more it becomes so, the more it ceases to be education and turns into propaganda and brainwashing, techniques obviously at odds with democracy. The teacher, while she or he may have great influence, is finally dependent upon the learner. The human being's extraordinary capacity for learning ultimately rests on the desire to do so. In the end, we learn what we want to learn, and if we choose not to, we can be quite successful at remaining ignorant.

Because no education is perfectly efficient and nor should it be, democracies tend to be more disorderly than their authoritarian counterparts. Democracies' natural tendency to be unsteady has been recognized in the empirical literature for some time. Even in the early 1980s, Richard Estes, in his *The Social Progress of Nations*, found that democracies were about 40 percent more likely to have demonstrations, strikes, riots, armed attacks, domestic violence, and so on than nondemocratic countries. Some disorder is part of the price of freedom.

For a society committed to the value of freedom the possibilities and rewards are great, but so are the risks and responsibilities. Much depends upon how freedom is understood. The more people tend to think of freedom only as being able to do whatever they want—the way that most Americans define it—the greater the risks to the society as a whole. The risks are both short- and long-term. The short-term risks are of random eruptions of chaos in the form of dysfunctional behavior at one extreme and violence at the other. The long-term risk is the demise of democracy itself.

Thinkers, both ancient and modern, and as disparate as Noam Chomsky on the Left and Allan Bloom on the Right, agree on this point: the central task of any education worthy of the name is to teach people how to be free. However, the requisite lesson cannot have as its objective an indiscriminate, egoistic freedom that knows few limits. It rather must aim to achieve autonomy, which is itself a kind of balance between a disposition to challenge limits on the one hand, and to respect them on the other.

Autonomy's lesson is among the most difficult to teach and digest for there is much in a modern democratic culture that conspires against it. For one thing, advanced capitalist democratic cultures have a tendency to "normalize deviance." By this we mean they make extreme cases appear to be normal when in fact they deviate far from the norm. It does this, to give one example, by often presenting on mainstream television individuals who behave in extreme and bizarre ways, behavior which, precisely because it is displayed on mainstream television, entices children to easily mistake it for the norm rather than the exception.

As adults, we may too easily forget that earlier time in our lives when the most pressing question for us was, "Who am I?"; a question that—especially in a free society—typically occupies every young person's thoughts. But in struggling with this question, the young perforce confronts another: "What does it mean to be a human being?," for this is what we are.

As the life and social sciences teach us, we cannot adequately address the question of what it means to be human without some idea of the extremes and the average in between. Humans beings are the "becoming beings," to use Nietzsche's phrase, the beings with the capacity—God-given or not—of ratcheting ourselves up ever higher on the evolutionary ladder.

What we can do and be is not determined for us at birth as it is with other animals. Nonetheless, at any given moment, there are limits, and knowing what they are, knowing what is extreme and what is not, allows us to know ourselves and our culture and thereby gives us a chance of becoming free.

Becoming free means, as the Delphic Oracle told us, knowing ourselves, having our own thoughts as opposed to having others think for us. Freedom exists not only or even for the most part in the absence of restriction on our physical movements but mainly in our thoughts. It is freedom of mind, as Tocqueville reminded us, that democratic culture primarily assails.

Children growing up in a modern democracy daily get from television, the Internet, and the entertainment industry a set of images of what they should try to make of themselves, and of how they should think and feel about others and their relationships with them. These virtual experiences often tempt children, when they try to understand themselves—as they are naturally want to do—to think only of others and their opinions as opposed to looking within themselves as a source of direction. It also tends to encourage them, when dealing with others, to think only of themselves. Thus, the culture reinforces the radical individualism that Tocqueville and his social science successors feared, undermines trust, and teaches children to treat others as means to their own ends as opposed to ends in themselves—ways of behaving that correlate with unfreedom.[1]

Not all children, of course, succumb to the extremes of a democratic culture nor is every child's sense of self necessarily formed by it. But many do succumb. It is for these children, especially, that teachers' values are important as they impose limits on indiscriminate self-expression and freedom, and counteract the corrosive effects on community of the radical individualism that the culture cultivates.

In modern democracies, then, schools in general, and elementary- and secondary-school teachers in particular, teach children the limits of freedom. Thus, in striking the balance between freedom and order in our classrooms and schools today, educators in no small sense strike the balance for society as a whole, for they are conveying to children a sense of freedom's limits in a culture that knows fewer and fewer limits.

There is always the danger, of course, that the balance between freedom and order will be struck too far in the direction of order and away from freedom. That it has been so struck is, of course, a central proposition of the critique of schooling from the Left in America. Samuel Bowles and Herbert Gintis' *Schooling in Capitalist America*, Michael Katz' *The Irony of Early School Reform* and the work of later "revisionists" historians, Michael Apple's many works on education, ideology, and power, Noam Chomsky's *Chomsky on Mis-education*, as well as numerous other Left-leaning thinkers have in common the belief that American schools and schooling are too authoritarian and oppressive and systematically perpetuate a class structure that protects the power of elites.

Whatever truth there is in the Left's critique of American schools and schooling, it feeds on inequality. Whether we like it or not, the Left's case grows stronger the more that inequality grows in American society and its schools. So, those who would have the Left disappear, or at least be more quiet, need simply to address the imbalanced economy in ways that reduce inequality. A democracy, a society committed to the democratic ideal as its main organizing principle, needs opposition from within to counterbalance the forces of inequality, no matter how uncomfortable the opposition may make us feel.

The Left, however, goes too far and contributes to imbalance when its critique—as Richard Rorty suggests in his *Achieving Our Country*—destroys the willingness and capacity for a democracy's citizens to commit and attach themselves to their country's best ideals so that may be moved to correct its worst behaviors.

The task of ensuring that the freedom–order balance is struck, at any given moment, within the range that moves the democracy toward greater equality and freedom with responsibility—this task, to repeat, falls to leadership. The leadership responsibility, moreover, resides not simply at the top levels of the society but includes "systemic leadership," leaders everywhere throughout the entire system and its constituent organizations and institutions.[2]

BOLSTERING TRUST AND THE OTHER SOCIAL VALUES

Another important balance that must be struck in democratic societies is that between faith and reason or, what amounts to the same thing, between religion and science. While the United States is not the most religious society in the world—Iraq, Egypt, and Jordan are much more so—it is, after Brazil, one of the most religious in Christendom. Accordingly, the balance between religion and science is more central than it may be in other democracies.

In its purest form, this tension is between religion and science. But balance plays out in various guises at different levels of the society: faith and reason, belief and skepticism, trust and suspicion, confidence and doubt, and so on.

If the nineteenth century gave rise to philosophies that claimed science would replace religion as the primary guide for human behavior, the twentieth century showed religion and science to be at a standoff. In our own time, we are seeing that science did not kill God after all, as Karl Marx thought it should and Friedrich Nietzsche believed it did. The conflict between the two seems rather to have given rise to a host of little gods, as Max Weber predicted it would.

The little gods that plague American politics and culture today are fanatical beliefs that show neither the restraints of religion nor the rationality of values. They are obsessively held, and their adherents stubbornly refuse to admit compromise, the sine qua non of democracy, and without which, as Tocqueville suggested, democracy turns self-destructive.

The struggle to reconcile this tension is ongoing and manifests itself in the schools in a variety of forms not the least of which, as we have already discussed in previous chapters, is the controversies over school prayer and the teaching of creationism.

IMBALANCES IN THE SCHOOLS

Democracies, then, tend to emphasize freedom over order and reason over faith. These two balances are central in a democracy's value system. Imbalances in either tend to trigger further imbalances in other sectors of the society and within the democracy's constituent institutions. Among these institutions are, of course, educational institutions.

Science versus the Arts

With schools, the imbalances in the larger society tend to play out in the schools in the form of correlated imbalances. There are, for example, the imbalances that are created by an excessive emphasis in the broader culture on reason and rationality. One of these is an overemphasis on developing children's cognitive abilities at the expense of their aesthetic sensibilities or, put more simply, the imbalance between science and the arts.

One of the educational offshoots of these larger imbalances in the democratic society at large is the schools' tendency to overemphasize science and mathematics and to underemphasize the arts and children's aesthetic development. It is well known that when schools are faced with tight budgets and have to make cuts, the first things that are often to go are the arts. There is a growing research literature that suggests, however, that science and mathematics education is better when children are exposed to the arts.

Having said this, however, we cannot ignore the general findings from chapter 8: a small but significant proportion of American school teachers apparently lack some very basic science knowledge. So basic, in fact, is the knowledge they seem to lack that further research on the matter is warranted. If further investigation results in findings consistent with those reported here, then some solution—professional development or whatever—is urgently needed to address the problem. Whatever stabilizing effect teachers may have on democracy is diminished by their incapacity to provide students an accurate picture of science, as science and technology are two of modern democracy's driving forces.

Academic versus Vocational Education

One of the great imbalances in our modern school system is the one we have created between academic and vocational education, an imbalance due in no small degree to an exaggeration of the importance of theoretical reason and cognitive development over practical reason.

We create this imbalance by privileging academic work over vocational work. We praise the former and condemn with faint praise the latter. As a result, we lose the talent that we would gain by allowing college-tracked students to experience vocational education, and we lose the talent we would have if vocationally inclined students were allowed to pursue college after going through a vocational curriculum.

One upshot of this imbalance for our modern economies is that our colleges are producing students who cannot find gainful employment, and too many companies cannot find skilled workers.

THE IMBALANCED SOCIETY

If Tocqueville were alive today, he might come bearing bad news and good news. The bad news would be that we have managed to make ourselves into imbalanced societies, and perhaps nowhere is this more the case than in the United States, a nation already prone to extremes and exceptionalism.[3]

The good news, on the other hand, is that imbalances, if recognized, can be corrected. All it takes is leadership. It was Tocqueville, in fact, who said that the first task of leadership in a democracy is to "educate democracy." By this we take him to mean that one of the most important things that leadership can do in a democracy is to recognize its imbalances, to get others to recognize them, and to marshal collective effort to correct them.

Our teachers today are providing a leadership of their own, a moral leadership that helps steady our democracies. Their work today is being judged mainly by how well they convey to children the knowledge they need to pass high-stakes tests in science, mathematics, reading, and social studies. But this is not the only work they do in our fragile, modernity-swept democratic societies.

Teachers are reservoirs of trust for America. They are, as a group, more trusting than most Americans, for education and trust are highly correlated and most Americans have only a high-school education or less while most teachers have at least a bachelor's degree, and many of them also have graduate degrees.

Only the most highly educated Americans—those with four-year degrees or higher—are as trusting as teachers. But teachers are the only highly educated adults who come into prolonged and intense contact with all of our children, and come into contact with them when they are at their youngest and most impressionable.

Accordingly, teachers serve as role models of trust for the nation's children. To use a phrase that is now fashionable but to use it with a broader meaning than current usage has it, we can say that teachers "add value" to our children but the value they add is not just confined to their ability to pass tests but also to their willingness and capacity to trust. As we have seen, our children's trust levels stand to influence America's economic growth, among other things.

Teaching brings teachers into contact with students in ways and for purposes unknown in any other line of work. The intensity—the frequency and duration—of the relationship between teachers and their students is unique; by the time their K–12 education is done, students will typically have spent more than 16,000 hours of their lives in contact with their teachers. The time spent aims to develop not only their intellectual side but their moral capacity as well. Children in schools are not only instructed on how to read, do mathematics, and understand science. They are also taught to regard themselves, consider others, feel a sense of responsibility, and meet their obligations.

The "moral apprenticeship" that our children receive in our K–12 schools, teaches them, unconsciously as much as consciously, how and where to strike balances of various sorts: balances between self and others, freedom and control, work and play, obeying and questioning, putting things off and doing them immediately, working independently and in groups, being smart and being good. What is taught is a general moral sense of where to strike these balances and the habit of doing so.

The moral lessons that teachers provide our children are taught as much by precept as by example. Students observe how teachers regard themselves, and deal with others. They note where they are consistent and when they are not. They hear what they say and compare it with what they do. Our teachers have a profound impact on our children's moral development.

Teachers are among our unsteady democracies' greatest benefactors. They serve to check our natural tendency to leap into change before we look, and they serve as well as critical reservoirs of trust, helpfulness, cooperation, and fairness. Without our teachers' values to temper our excesses and to counteract our tendencies toward dissolution, our children would not only suffer badly but democracy in America would itself be more at risk. We forget this at our own peril.

NOTES

1. Robert N. Bellah, Richard Madsen, William Sullivan, Ann Swidler, Stephen M. Tipton, *Habits of the Heart: Individualism and Commitment in American Life* (Berkeley: University of California Press, 1985).

2. See Gary Crow and Robert Slater, *Educating Democracy* (Washington, DC: National Policy Board for Educational Administration, 1996).

3. See Seymour Martin Lipset, *American Exceptionalism* (New York: Norton, 1996).

Appendix

Table A3.1. Logistic Regression of Premarital Sex Is "Always Wrong" against Teachers and Other Predictors

	B	SE(B)	Exp (B)	T-Statistic	Probability
Teachers	.320	.122	1.378	2.634	.009
Gender	.159	.047	1.172	3.368	.001
Age	.030	.002	1.030	16.803	.000
Education	−.141	.009	.868	−15.800	.000
Race	−.347	.068	.707	−5.122	.000
Church Attendance	.492	.010	1.636	49.820	.000
Income	−.659	.475	.517	−1.387	.166
Region	.669	.180	.106	−12.516	.000
Pseudo R-square = .285		Adjusted Wald F = 365.798		p = .000	

Note: The Logit or premarital sex is "always wrong" is coded: 0 = "not wrong at all"; 1 = "always wrong"; predictor variables coded as follows: "Teachers": 0 = Nonteachers, 1 = Teachers; Gender: 1 = M, 2 = F; Age: 18–89+; "Education": 0–20 years; Race: 1 = White, 2 = Black; "Church Attendance": 0 to 8 where 0 = Never and 8 = More than once a week; "Income" respondent's income adjusted for inflation in 1986 dollars; "Region" is 9 U.S. Census Regions coded: 0 = 1–4, 8–9; 1 = 5–7 (the South).

Appendix

Table A3.2. Logistic Regression of "Had Sex Outside of Marriage" against Teachers and Other Predictors

	B	SE(B)	Exp (B)	T-Statistic	Probability
Teachers	−.595	.177	.552	−3.352	.001
Gender	−.199	.052	.820	−3.815	.001
Age	.038	002	1.039	19.657	.000
Education	−.015	.010	.985	−1.528	.127
Race	.337	.074	1.401	4.541	.000
Church Attendance	−089	.010	.915	−8.989	.000
Income	.031	..010	1.032	3.260	.001
Region	.175	.053	1.191	3.291	.001
Constant	−3.395	0.215	0.034	−15.773	000

Pseudo R-square = .285   Adjusted Wald F = 365.798   p = .000

Note: The Logit or "had sex outside of marriage" is coded: 0 = "no"; 1 = "yes"; predictor variables coded as follows: "Teachers": 0 = Nonteachers, 1 = Teachers; Gender: 1 = M, 2 = F; Age: 18–89+; "Education": 0–20 years; Race: 1 = White, 2 = Black; "Church Attendance": 0 to 8 where 0 = Never and 8 = More than once a week; "Income" respondent's income adjusted for inflation in 1986 dollars; "Region" is 9 U.S. Census Regions coded: 0 = 1–4, 8–9; 1 = 5–7 (the South).

Table A3.3. Logistic Regression of "Favor Sex Education in the Public Schools" on Teachers and Other Predictors

	B	SE(B)	Exp (B)	T-Statistic	Probability
Teachers	−.465	.142	.628	−3.270	.000
Gender	.503	.056	1.653	9.027	.000
Age	−.023	.002	.977	−12.214	.000
Education	.146	.009	1.157	15.605	.000
Race	.075	.049	1.078	1.512	.131
Church Attendance	−.227	.010	.797	−22.203	.000
Income	.230	.057	1.259	4.032	.000
Region	−.233	.052	.792	−4.439	.000
Constant	1.399	0.183	4.050	7.629	000

Pseudo R-square = .10   Adjusted Wald F = 138.354   p = .000

Note: The Logit or "favor sex education in public schools" is coded: 0 = "oppose"; 1 = "favor"; predictor variables coded as follows: "Teachers": 0 = Nonteachers, 1 = Teachers; Gender: 1 = M, 2 = F; Age: 18–89+; "Education": 0–20 years; Race: 1 = White, 2 = Black; "Church Attendance": 0 to 8 where 0 = Never and 8 = More than once a week; "Income" respondent's income adjusted for inflation in 1986 dollars; "Region" is 9 U.S. Census Regions coded: 0 = 1–4, 8–9; 1 = 5–7 (the South).

Table A3.4. Logistic Regression of "Allow a Woman an Abortion for Any Reason" on Teachers and Other Predictors

	B	SE(B)	Exp (B)	T-Statistic	Probability
Teachers	−.251	.086	.778	−2.927	.004
Gender	.282	.032	1.325	8.665	.000
Age	.002	001	1.002	12.96	.195
Education	.171	.006	1.186	26.905	.000
Race	−.009	.030	.991	−.294	.769
Church Attendance	−.263	.006	.768	−41.303	.000
Income	.017	.005	1.017	3.337	.001
Region	−.208	.033	.812	−6.321	.000
Constant	**−2.166**	**0.166**	**0.115**	**−18.608**	**000**
Pseudo R-square = .11		Adjusted Wald F = 294.473		p = .000	

Note: The Logit or "allow a woman an abortion for any reason" is coded: 0 = "no"; 1 = "yes"; predictor variables coded as follows: "Teachers": 0 = Nonteachers, 1 = Teachers; Gender: 1 = M, 2 = F; Age: 18–89+; "Education": 0–20 years; Race: 1 = White, 2 = Black; "Church Attendance": 0 to 8 where 0 = Never and 8 = More than once a week; "Income" respondent's income adjusted for inflation in 1986 dollars; "Region" is 9 U.S. Census Regions coded: 0 = 1–4, 8–9; 1 = 5-7 (the South).

Table A4.1. Logistic Regression of Predictors of Attending Church One or More Times per Week (1972–2012)

	B	SE(B)	Exp (B)	T-Statistic	Probability
Teachers	.337	.069	1.401	4.861	.000
Gender	.245	.030	1.278	8.280	.000
Age	.025	.001	1.025	23.182	.000
Education	.076	.007	1.079	13.541	.000
Region	.232	.030	1.261	7.714	.000
Income	−.039	.005	.962	−8.219	.000
Race	.226	.042	1.254	5.347	.000
Catholic	.191	.032	1.211	6.042	.000
Year	−.007	.001	.993	−5.149	.000
Constant	**11.476**	**28.43**	**96,407.112**	**40.37**	**.000**
Pseudo R-square = .03			p = .00		

Note: The Logit or "attending church one or more times per week" is coded: 0 = "less than one or more times per week"; 1= "one or more times per week"; predictor variables coded as follows: "Teachers": 0 = Nonteachers, 1 = Teachers; Gender: 1 = M, 2 = F; Age: 18–89+; "Education": 0–20 years; Race: 1 = White, 2 = Black; "Church Attendance": 0 to 8 where 0 = Never and 8 = More than once a week; "Income" respondent's income adjusted for inflation in 1986 dollars; "Region" is 9 U.S. Census Regions coded: 0 = 1–4, 8–9; 1 = 5-7 (the South); "Catholic" 0 = "Protestant", 1 = "Catholic"; "year": 1972–2012.

Table A4.2. Logistic Regression of Predictors of Praying One or More Times per Day (2010–2012)

	B	SE(B)	Exp (B)	T-Statistic	Probability
Teachers	.242	.106	1.274	2.282	.023
Gender	.776	.039	2.172	19.760	.000
Age	.028	.001	1.028	19.364	.000
Education	.029	.007	1.029	3.925	.000
Region	.410	.040	1.507	10.286	.000
Income	−.127	.041	.881	−3.060	.002
Race	.906	.062	2.476	14.594	.000
Catholic	−.085	.041	.919	−2.054	.041
Constant	−3.389	.159	.034	−21.342	.000
	Pseudo R-square = .07		p = .00		

Note: The Logit or "praying one or more times per day" is coded: 0 = "less than one or more times per day"; 1 = "one or more times per day"; predictor variables coded as follows: "Teachers": 0 = Nonteachers, 1 = Teachers; Gender: 1 = M, 2 = F; Age: 18–89+; "Education": 0–20 years; Race: 1 = White, 2 = Black; "Church Attendance": 0 to 8 where 0 = Never and 8 = More than once a week; "Income" respondent's income adjusted for inflation in 1986 dollars; "Region" is 9 U.S. Census Regions coded: 0 = 1–4, 8–9; 1 = 5–7 (the South).

Table A6.1. Logistic Regression of Highly Supportive of Freespeech against Being a Teacher, Education, Gender, Class, Race, Religion, and Region.

Teachers, African Americans, frequent church goers and Southerners tend to be less supportive of free speech than non-teachers, Whites, those who attend church less often and Americans not living in the South. Also, the more education Americans have, the more they tend to support free speech.

	B	SE(B)	T-Statistic	Probability
Teachers	−.42	.098	−4.261	.000
Education	.30	.008	37.339	.000
Gender	.02	.037	.544	.587
Income	.05	.038	1.266	.206
Race	−.27	.056	−4.743	.000
Church Attendance	−.14	.007	20.917	.000
Region	−.40	.037	−10.845	.000
Constant	−2.96	.131	−22.677	.000
	Pseudo R square = .12			

Note: The Logit or "high support of free speech" is coded: 0= "9 or less on 12-point free-speech scale"; 1= "10-12 on free speech scale"; Predictor variables coded as follows: "Teachers" : 0=non-teachers, 1=Teachers; Gender: 1= M, 2 = F; Age: 18-89+; "Education": 0-20 years; Race: 1=White, 2=Black;"Income" respondent's income adjusted for inflation in 1986 dollars; "attendance": 0=attend church less than once a week, 1=attend church one or more times per week; "Region" is 9 U.S. Census Regions coded: 0 = 1-4,8-9; 1 = 5-7 (the South).

Index

About the Author

Robert Slater holds a master's degree from Harvard University and a PhD from the University of Chicago. A Senior Fulbright Scholar to Peru in 1996, and again to Bolivia 2010, his teaching, research, and writing focuses on education and the vicissitudes of democracy. He is professor of education at the University of Louisiana at Lafayette where he directs the doctoral program in educational leadership..

Made in the USA
Lexington, KY
12 January 2018

Education • Philosophy and Social Aspects

"This elegantly written book is a profound philosophical analysis of the values that American teachers espouse. Based on vast statistical data, Robert Slater explores the current beliefs and attitudes of U.S. school teachers and poses many questions, including the following: What values do American teachers hold? How do they teach these values? Is freedom among the values they teach? Some readers may disagree with the author's conclusions. In fact, some readers may even dislike these conclusions; however, the controversies this book stirs up are the result of exploring the uncharted areas in U.S. school education. Besides being a great read, *The Values of American Teachers* offers fresh and original strokes to the portrait of the contemporary American teacher." —**Pavel Samsonov**, Slimco/BORSF endowed professor, University of Louisiana at Lafayette

Education today is increasingly focused on tests and testing. Teachers are being judged on how much they can increase test scores from one year to the next. These year-to-year gains in scores are part of a "value-added" approach to teacher evaluation, and value-added teacher assessment is all the rage now. A main point of this book is that while teachers do add value when they enable students to increase their performance on standardized tests, this is neither the only nor the most important value they add. An analysis of 40 years of data on teachers suggests that an equally if not more important value added is their contribution to the stability of our increasingly unsteady democracy. Teachers help steady modern democracy by teaching children the limits of liberty and by cultivating the social virtues—trust, cooperation, helpfulness, and the like—upon which civil society depends. We need not only to recognize this but also to avoid education policies that undermine their willingness and ability to do so.

ROBERT SLATER holds a master's degree from Harvard University and a PhD from the University of Chicago. A Senior Fulbright Scholar to Peru in 1996, and again to Bolivia in 2010, his teaching, research, and writing focus on education and the vicissitudes of democracy. He is professor of education at the University of Louisiana at Lafayette, where he directs the doctoral program in educational leadership.

ROWMAN & LITTLEFIELD EDUCATION
A division of Rowman & Littlefield
800-462-6420 • www.rowman.com

ISBN 978-1-4758-0007-4

9 781475 800074